gestalten

For more information,
please visit *gestalten.com*
———

Bibliographic information
published by the Deutsche
Nationalbibliothek: The Deutsche
Nationalbibliothek lists this
publication in the Deutsche
Nationalbibliografie; detailed
bibliographic data are available
online at *dnb.d-nb.de*

This book was printed on
paper certified by the FSC®

Monocle editor in chief
and chairman: *Tyler Brûlé*
Monocle editor: *Andrew Tuck*
Books editor: *Joe Pickard*
Guide editor: *Melkon Charchoglyan*
———

Designed by *Monocle*
Proofreading by *Monocle*
Typeset in *Plantin & Helvetica*
———

Printed by *Offsetdruckerei
Grammlich, Pliezhausen*

Made in Germany

Published by *gestalten*, Berlin 2019
ISBN 978-3-89955-972-9

© Die Gestalten Verlag GmbH &
Co. KG, Berlin 2019

The MONOCLE
Travel Guide Series

39

Marrakech
Tangier + Casablanca

Contents
———
Marrakech
Tangier +
Casablanca

Use the key below to help navigate the guide section by section.

 H Hotels

F Food and drink

R Retail

C Culture

D Design and architecture

S Sport and fitness

W Walks

B Best of the rest

T Things we'd buy

E Essays

Tangier

Casablanca

Marrakech

Eenie, meenie, miney, mo. Marrakech is brimming with places to go and people to see. The choice is yours!

Welcome
—— Made in Morocco

Labyrinthine alleyways piled high with luminous glassware, pungent spices and handwoven rugs. Tooting mopeds, clickety horse and carts, and the muezzin's call to prayer. Marrakech is a *feast for the senses* – and yet, amid what can feel like chaos, there are *pockets of calm*. Tucked away behind intricately carved wooden doors you'll find tranquil riads and verdant gardens.

Marrakech can feel like the city that time forgot but the sands are starting to shift. The opening of the Macaal museum in 2006 heralded a new era for *African art* and the addition of the Musée Yves Saint Laurent in 2017 provided the city with a much-needed dose of contemporary architecture. Today commercial-art galleries stand alongside *16th-century palaces* and avant garde fashion boutiques rub shoulders with family-run stalls in the *souks*. International flavours mingle with traditional Moroccan cuisine and the hotel scene is booming – plush pads are more plentiful here than in most major cities around the world.

Like the medina, the history of Marrakech is full of *twists and turns*. Morocco's "Jewel of the South" was founded in 1062 and served as the capital several times before that role went to Rabat. Its Moorish roots continue to shine through, though the 45 years of French rule between 1912 and 1956 left their mark – after Arabic, French is the second most widely spoken language.

Marrakech has long attracted a *curious crowd* and is now one of the most popular destinations on the continent. Keep your wits about you, yes, but more importantly keep your eyes peeled for hidden treasures. — (M)

Map
—— Way to go

At first glance, Marrakech can look like a hot mess. How does anyone find their way around? It can help to get to know the city's main neighbourhoods.

First there's the medina (old town), which is where you'll find souks, rooftop cafés, opulent riads and verdant courtyards behind ornate wooden doors. Sure, it will take time for you to get your bearings – there are many intricate alleyways that aren't mapped by Google and often come to dead ends. But follow your feet – and, perhaps, ask a street vendor or two – and eventually you'll find your way back to Jemaa El Fna (the central square) or the main road, fringed by the old city ramparts.

West of the medina is Hivernage: a broad, upscale neighbourhood of flashy nightclubs and fortress-like resorts. Meanwhile, northwest is Gueliz (the new town), which was built by the French when Morocco was a protectorate between 1912 and 1956. The streets here are wider, the shops contemporary and the atmosphere more laissez-faire – which is to say you'll find plenty of establishments willing to serve you a cold beer.

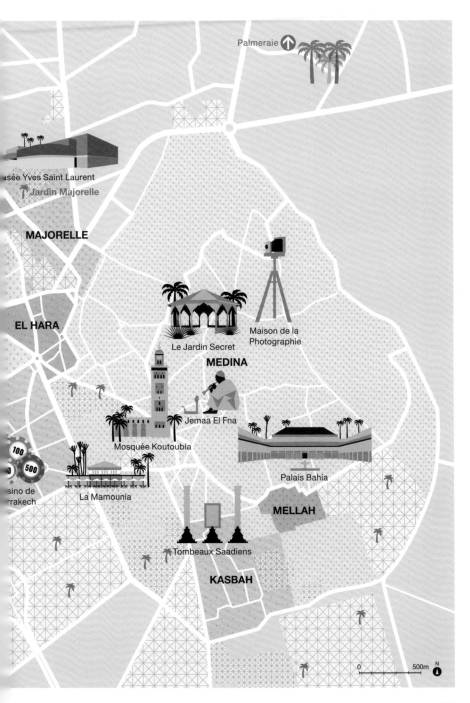

Palmeraie

Musée Yves Saint Laurent

Jardin Majorelle

MAJORELLE

EL HARA

Maison de la
Photographie

Le Jardin Secret

MEDINA

Jemaa El Fna

Mosquée Koutoubia

Palais Bahia

Casino de
Marrakech

La Mamounia

MELLAH

Tombeaux Saadiens

KASBAH

0   500m

Need to know
—— Get to grips with the basics

Raising a glass
Alcohol

Alcohol is *haram* (forbidden) in Islam but in Marrakech, and Morocco generally, it's fine for foreigners to drink and most hotels serve alcohol. The only real dry zone is the conservative medina (old town). Only a handful of restaurants here have licenses to serve booze and there are no corner shops or supermarkets selling it (don't even dream of drinking on the street). But once you're in Gueliz or Hivernage, which are much more liberal (and popular with expats), you'll find plenty of bars, clubs and bottle shops.

National voices
Language

The native tongue of Morocco is Darija, a dialect of Arabic that's heavily influenced by Berber – the language of the indigenous Berber people of north Africa. But as Morocco was a French protectorate from 1912 to 1956, the country has maintained the tradition of teaching French in schools as a second language – so French will get you further than English.

Sacred duty
Religion

Morocco is a traditional Muslim country. Five times a day – and yes, during the night – a *muezzin* (summoner) shouts the *Adhan* (call to prayer) from every minaret in town. Homosexuality is illegal and, though the law doesn't apply to foreigners, it's best not to display signs of same-sex affection (though ironically it's common here for two men to hold hands if they're friends). Conservative dress isn't obligatory but women should avoid short skirts and revealing tops, as this will result in unwanted attention *(see page 128)*.

Food for thought
Hygiene

Moroccan cuisine is hearty, heavy on the spices and generally delicious. But this country, and Marrakech in particular, is also renowned for food poisoning as hygiene standards are often low. Have no fear while eating at restaurants but be careful when it comes to street food. If a stall isn't busy, or the cook doesn't seem to care about the flies hovering above the meat, then it's best to move on. Carrying a bottle of hand-sanitiser is also a good idea. For peace of mind, follow our food and drink tips *(see pages 42 to 43)*.

Mmm, I wonder if I can recreate this at home....

Display of gratitude
Tipping

The rule of thumb is to tip 15 to 20 per cent in restaurants, particularly for dinner and if the service has been good. Don't feel obliged to leave anything at street stalls or after a simple lunch – tips are a sign of thanks rather than an essential part of the staff's salary as, say, in the US. Note that some restaurants add the service automatically while others don't, so be sure to check your bill.

I'm a discerning traveller, can't you see?

Strike a deal
Haggling

Morocco is one eternal hustle. People bargain for everything in an endless cycle of feigned indignation, arm throwing and number crunching. But at the end of the day everyone emerges as friends – it's just part of the culture. In most transactions, bargaining is also a sign of respect, as it suggests that *you* really want the thing: to not haggle over a sizeable purchase in a souk would be an insult to the salesman's wares. There's an art to it all, the mysteries of which we've handily unravelled in one of our essays *(see page 126)*.

Well hailed
Taxis

Taxi drivers are notorious for triple or quadruple charging foreigners. Request that the meter is turned on or settle on a price before you hop in. A trip from the medina to Gueliz should be about 15MAD – so you can extrapolate other fares based on that. Many drivers will simply drive off and you may have to repeat the negotiating process before someone agrees to take you. If you hail a car on the street, don't be surprised if you find another passenger inside – the driver will take you too if you're heading in the same direction.

We suggest you download a ride app called Roby, which is used by the regular licensed taxis. It will avoid you a lot of headaches since the price is set. Just make sure you have Whatsapp installed on your phone – that's how the driver will let you know they've arrived.

Navigating the labyrinth
Getting around

Getting lost in the medina is part of the fun of Marrakech. Besides, you'll always find your way out. Google Maps has done a decent job of mapping the larger streets but the warren of covered alleyways in the centre is a total enigma. House numbers and street names are often arbitrary – number three could easily be next to number 257. If you're lost or need help, ask a shopkeeper (women can be a little more reliable). And if you can't find a restaurant or shop that you're after, call and ask for directions.

I thought the medina was that way?

Royal rule
Monarchy

Morocco is an ancient kingdom dating back to 789AD and Marrakech served as the capital several times throughout its long history. Images of the current king, Mohammed VI, adorn most houses and establishments. It's not surprising then that the country enforces *lèse-majesté*: it's illegal to insult or defame the king (though some "constructive criticism" in the press is allowed). Though Mohammed VI is more enlightened than his father, Hassan II – who violently cracked down on dissidents – the monarch is nothing short of a traditional autocrat. He often visits Marrakech too, staying in his palace near Dar el Bacha in the medina.

Protective behaviour
Safety

Marrakech is not, strictly speaking, dangerous but petty theft and harassment are rife. What tends to happen is a youth will shout that you're going the wrong way and that you must follow them – don't – or try to sell you hashish. Pickpockets are aplenty, as are thieves on scooters (so be vigilant when using your phone). It's also best not to walk around the Kasbah alone at night.

Our top picks:

01 **El Fenn:** A labyrinthine hotel with a first-rate rooftop restaurant.
see page 15

02 **Musée Yves Saint Laurent:** Couture meets contemporary architecture.
see pages 64 and 72-73

03 **Marrakshi Life:** Morocco's definitive fashion label.
see pages 46-47

04 **Palais Bahia:** *Bahia* translates as "beautiful" or "brilliant". Need we say more?
see page 76

05 **La Mamounia:** This opulent hotel boasts five bars and four restaurants.
see page 17

06 **Dar Cherifa:** A 16th-century riad that serves traditional dishes.
see page 27

07 **Maison de la Photographie:** More than 10,000 documents from 1870 to 1960.
see page 63

08 **Scarabeo Camp:** Dinner in the Agafay Desert.
see page 41

09 **Malakut:** Perfect ceramics in a pint-sized shop.
see page 54

10 **Terrasse des Épices:** Enjoy a bottle of rosé with a view of the medina.
see page 44

Make way, make way!

Hotels
—— Where to stay

Few cities can hold a candle to the glamour and diversity of Marrakech's hospitality offering.

Fancy bedding down in a grand hotel fit for – and built on the orders of – a king? If opulence is what you're after, Royal Mansour more than fits the bill. Over at La Mamounia, old-school grandeur is served in abundance while Amanjena is dripping with contemporary charm.

Perhaps you'd rather check into a traditional riad renovated by an international design icon? The classic Moroccan guesthouse experience doesn't get much better than Jasper Conran's L'Hôtel Marrakech. And that's not to mention the romantic camps in the star-filled desert.

Whatever your whim, you'll find an exotic and beautifully designed retreat to suit. Read on for our round-up of the very best places to rest your head.

Hotels
Luxury check-ins

1
Amanjena, Annakhil
Glamorous digs

Designed by US architect Ed Tuttle, Amanjena is an impressive collection of soaring rust-coloured pillars, turquoise tiles, shaded walkways, towering palm trees and jade pools. Opened in 2000 by luxury resort chain Aman, it benefits from a serene setting some 11km from the centre of Marrakech. (As you enter, look out for the water feature inspired by the Jardin Ménara.)

The rooms are spread across 32 pavilions and seven maisons – some of which include butler service. With tennis courts, a pool and three restaurants at your disposal, you'll need hardly leave.
KM12 Route de Ouarzazate
+212 (0)5 2439 9040
aman.com/amanjena

MONOCLE COMMENT: Take a break from tagines at Amanjena's Japanese restaurant where you can tuck into izakaya-style dishes.

②

El Fenn, Medina
Boutique beauty

This labyrinthine hotel comprises seven conjoined riads interspersed with bougainvillea-filled courtyards and shady terraces. Former British gallerist and Marrakech Biennale founder Vanessa Branson established El Fenn in 2004 and has filled it with an array of contemporary pieces from her own collection. Look out for the Francis Upritchard chandelier and a series of ink studies by Antony Gormley.

The sumptuous interiors are by Dutch designer Willem Smit, who combines lavish contemporary furnishings with traditional Moroccan touches such as carved wooden panels and colourfully tiled floors. Head to the rooftop restaurant (*see page 32*), which is also open to non-guests, for views over the Mosquée Koutoubia and Atlas Mountains.
2 Derb Moulay Abdullah Ben Hussain
+212 (0)5 2444 1210
el-fenn.com

MONOCLE COMMENT: Duck into the ground-floor shop for your pick of fashion, jewellery, homeware and more.

3

Royal Mansour, Medina
Grand flight of fancy

Truly a hotel fit for a king, Royal Mansour was built at the demand of King Mohammed VI who insisted that no expense be spared. The result is an astounding complex of 53 luxury riads, laid out in an imitation medina and connected by palm-tree-lined pathways.

Opened in 2010, the hotel is a veritable showpiece of Moroccan craftsmanship; more than 1,500 artisans worked to produce vast stretches of intricate mosaic and stuccowork, as well as handmade bronze and silver furniture. The three-storey riads are rented out individually and come with a butler, terrace and plunge pool.
Rue Abou El Abbas Sebti
+212 (0)5 2980 8080
royalmansour.com

MONOCLE COMMENT: The riads are connected by underground passages so staff can travel speedily between rooms unseen.

Day dipper
—

Some of the bigger hotels, including Royal Mansour and La Mamounia (*see opposite*), offer day passes for non-guests to use their pool. A little relaxation in a lounger can be a welcome respite when the chaos of the medina becomes overwhelming.

4

La Mamounia, Medina
Lavish ornamentation

This decadent hotel has been welcoming a star-studded clientele since opening in 1923 and is famously where Winston Churchill spent his winters. It's a celebration of art deco opulence combined with intricate Moorish details; every corner is decked out in *zellige* (patterned geometric mosaic tiling), *moucharabieh* (carved cedar screens) and *zouac* (brightly painted wooden panelling).

The 135-room institution is home to five bars, four restaurants and a sprawling garden. Guests looking to unwind can choose to relax by the vast outdoor pool, beneath the vaulted ceilings of an equally grand indoor pool, or in one of the three hammams housed in the underground spa (*see page 86*).
Avenue Bab Jdid
+212 (0)5 2438 8600
mamounia.com

MONOCLE COMMENT:
A clutch of pampered cats call La Mamounia's gardens home: keep an eye out for them having, ahem, a catnap in the flowerbeds.

❺

L'Hôtel Marrakech, Medina
Classy hideaway

Owned by British designer
Jasper Conran, L'Hôtel
Marrakech is a serene escape
close to the bustling Jemaa
El Fna square. The hotel is
housed in a 19th-century riad
originally built as the central
part of an ancient palace and
has retained a feeling of
regal elegance.

The high-ceilinged rooms
are adorned with elegant
antique furnishings and
artwork from Conran's
personal collection. Five suites
are positioned around a central
courtyard complete with a
turquoise-tiled pool shaded by
leafy lemon and banana trees
– all enchantingly lantern-
lit by night. Up on the roof,
breakfast, lunch and afternoon
tea are served in a curtained
pergola, surrounded by orange
and fig trees and with views
across the medina.
41 Derb Sidi Lahcen Ouest Ali
+212 (0)5 2438 7880
l-hotelmarrakech.com

MONOCLE COMMENT: Be
sure to check out the snug
1930s-style bar – the perfect
place to hide away with a
cocktail and a good book.

Riads
Traditional stays

①

Dar Kawa, Medina
Custom bolthole

With its chic monochrome tones, Dar Kawa is a modern update of the traditional riad. Owned by textile designer Valérie Barkowski, the hotel is charmingly decked out in her creations, from cushions and throws to hand-embroidered bed linen. Many of these designs are also available to buy so guests can take a little bit of the riad home with them.

"When I arrived in Marrakech in 1996 I fell in love with the traditional houses and architecture," says Barkowski, who spent three years renovating Dar Kawa before opening it as an intimate four-room guesthouse in 1999.
18 Derb Ouali
+212 (0)6 6134 4333
darkawa.net

MONOCLE COMMENT: The tiny riad can also be rented out as a whole for private use, so gather a gang for an exclusive getaway.

②

Riad Jardin Secret, Medina
Hidden gem

Riad Jardin Secret is owned by Parisian duo Julien Phomveha and Cyrielle Rigot, who left their jobs in the fashion industry to open the seven-room guesthouse in 2015. The couple are on hand most days to share tips with guests.

"The riad is from the late 16th century," says Rigot. "We renovated it while taking care to preserve its historical heritage." Today it's a riot of elaborate white stuccowork, stained-glass windows and wrought-iron balustrades set around a leafy courtyard.
43-46 Arset Aouzal
+212 (0)5 2437 6606
riadjardinsecret.com

MONOCLE COMMENT: Lunch and dinner, served on the rooftop, are wholly vegetarian and exclusive to riad guests.

❸
Riad Tizwa, Medina
Tasteful comfort

"The building has amazing original period details such as elaborate plaster work," says Richard Bee, who opened this homely six-room riad with his brother Daniel in 2006. "The walls are also up to 1.5-metres thick, which keeps rooms naturally cool in summer and warm in winter."

Breakfast is served on the large roof terrace, which is dotted with sunloungers, and includes a particularly delicious spread of semi-leavened bread, pancakes and homemade yoghurt.
26 Derb Gueraba
+44 (0)7973 115471
riadtizwa.com

MONOCLE COMMENT: The brothers own an equally excellent riad by the same name in Fez.

Three more

01 Riad 72, Medina: This six-room guesthouse comes with all the mod cons while maintaining a traditional charm. The on-site restaurant La Table du Riad is also worth a visit for modern updates of classic dishes. *riad72.com*

02 Riad Be, Medina: Almost every surface of this 10-room stop-in is covered in colourful tiles. There's also a hammam and cookery courses on offer. *be-marrakech.com*

03 Riad Mena, Medina: With interiors from Swiss interior designer Romain Michel Menière, this is a sleek oasis within the medina. Its six rooms are decorated in a style reminiscent of 1960s Marrakech. *riadmenaandbeyond.com*

It's not high tea but I'll take it

4

Riad Numa, Medina
Chic retreat

You'll find this bright-and-breezy bolthole tucked away down a winding, narrow alleyway in the medina. Opened by Milanese couple Mauro Violini and Claudia Amadeo (*both pictured*) in 2018, the guesthouse revolves around a leafy courtyard with tall whitewashed walls and a giant outdoor fireplace.

"We wanted our riad to be contemporary but not cold," says Mauro. "When decorating, we drew on our love for design and tried to use as many local materials as possible." The result is a well-turned-out set of six rooms featuring an intriguing mix of modern furnishings and traditional Moorish touches such as carved stucco ceilings and stained-glass windows.
37 Derb Aarjan
+212 (0)8 0852 1050
numamarrakech.com

MONOCLE COMMENT: You'll want to spend some time cooling off in the neatly designed pool, which is positioned on a mezzanine over the courtyard.

Out of town
Escape the ordinary

1

Scarabeo Camp, Agafay Desert
Pitch perfect

In the Agafay, a rocky desert 35km outside Marrakech, Scarabeo Camp boasts 360-degree views across the dusty, rolling landscape and the Atlas Mountains beyond. The camp, however, is perhaps at its most spectacular by night when it's lit by lanterns, and guests gather around open fires.

There are 15 breezy tents decorated with Berber rugs, handwoven bedspreads and antique furnishings, plus dining tents. We'd recommend coming for lunch or dinner (*see page 41*) whether or not you plan to stay the night.
Agafay Desert
+212 (0)5 2420 1117
scarabeocamp.com

MONOCLE COMMENT: Be sure to experience the desert on one of the offered camel rides.

2

Berber Lodge, Oumnas
Contemporary meets traditional

A dusty, nameless track leads to this nine-lodge complex founded in 2017 by Swiss interior designer Romain Michel Menière, the eye behind projects such as Nomad (*see page 30*). The buildings are designed in the style of traditional Berber residences using natural materials including mud bricks, bamboo and palm-tree trunks. The rustic, earthy palette is pepped up by contemporary touches such as Achille Castiglioni resin lamps and curiosities sourced by Menière on his travels.
Douar Oumnes, Tamesloth
+212 (0)6 6204 9043
berberlodge.net

MONOCLE COMMENT:
The complex is built around a central swimming pool and an old olive grove.

❸

Kasbah Bab Ourika, Ourika Valley
Scenic outlook

Kasbah Bab Ourika prides itself on the exceptional views it offers over the Ourika Valley to the mountain peaks beyond. The 28-room hotel is built from the traditional Berber building material pisé (coral-coloured clay) and has large outdoor terraces with winding pathways leading down to a walled pool. There is also a verdant vegetable garden where organic produce is grown for use in the kitchen.
Ourika Valley, Tnine Ourika
+212 (0)6 6874 9547
kasbahbabourika.com

MONOCLE COMMENT: Opt for a room in the small villa at the foot of the garden. It has its own infinity pool overlooking the valley and a sliding glass roof for stargazing.

Food and drink
—— Spicy bites

In a few short years, Marrakech's food scene has transformed from one heavy with traditional *prix fixe* menus in stuffy settings to something altogether more diverse, colourful and multicultural. Of course the fine old Moroccan institutions are kicking on but they've been joined by a host of more unexpected options, such as modern Australian joints, restaurants purveying Senegalese and Lebanese flavours, and Italian and French fine-dining establishments.

At the heart of everything – no matter the cuisine – you'll find fresh ingredients sourced from the varied and fertile landscapes of Morocco: think oysters from the Atlantic, Agadir tangerines and lamb from the Atlas Mountains. There are even wineries producing fine vintages, as unlikely as that might seem.

Adding to your dining pleasure are a wealth of picturesque settings: take your pick from Marrakshi rooftops, leafy courtyards, desert camps and an ancient palace.

Dinner
Top tables

①
Le Jardin Marrakech, Medina
Cool retreat

This garden restaurant attracts a chic crowd with its breezy 1970s-style decor, designed by interior architect Anne Favier, and menu of both Moroccan and western-style dishes. It's part of Kamal Laftimi's hip stable, which also includes Nomad (*see page 30*), Café des Épices (*see page 38*) and ChiChaoua Tea Room (*see page 39*).

The vegetarian options in particular capitalise on regional produce: standouts include the carrot hummus with paprika and courgette-and-feta fritters.
32 Souk Sidi Abdelaziz
+212 (0)5 2437 8295
lejardinmarrakech.com

❷

Dar Cherifa, Medina
Romantic and intimate

As soon as you step into this riad's high-walled 16th-century courtyard, the clamour of the medina feels a world away. It serves a simple à la carte menu and excels in *tanjias* (couscous-laden stews, whether with meat or vegetables). Tables are few and generously spaced, making for an intimate environment, plus there's a shady rooftop.
8 Derb Chorfa Lakbir
+212 (0)5 2442 6550
marrakech-riads.com/restaurant-dar-cherifa

To Dar Cherifa!

Mes'Lalla, Annakhil
Elegant balance

Tucked away inside the
Mandarin Oriental, this is
the place to go if you fancy
an upscale Moroccan feast.
(Admittedly the menu also
features international dishes
but we recommend sticking
to the local selection).

Happily, chef Cédric
D'Ambrosio hasn't followed
the trend of upsetting age-old
Moroccan flavour balances
for the sake of novelty. Produce
is sourced from the on-site
vegetable garden and the
lemon-chicken tagine is one
of the finest around.
Route Golf Royal
+212 (0)5 2429 8888
mandarinoriental.com/marrakech

Simple pleasures

The ingredients for the
ubiquitous egg-and-potato
sandwich may be simple
but don't be deceived:
this soft-white-roll snack is
elevated by a drizzle of olive
oil, a sprinkle of cumin and a
dollop of harissa. You'll see
stands selling it throughout
the medina.

⑤ Al Fassia, Gueliz
Family affair

Sisters Myra and Saïda Chab have created a mainstay of the Gueliz hospitality scene, one that feels more akin to dining in a welcoming Moroccan home than a restaurant. The decor may be a little staid but that's all part of the experience.

Al Fassia is famed for its lamb shoulder; in fact, the dish is so popular it's best to request it upon making a reservation. The selection of no fewer than 15 starter salads will keep vegetarians happy too.

The sisters also have a second restaurant near the Jardins d'Agdal if you can't reserve a table at the original Gueliz outpost.
55 Boulevard Mohammed Zerktouni
+212 (0)5 2443 4060
alfassia.com

④ Grand Café de la Poste, Gueliz
Warm welcome

This opulently old-world venue is an institution and offers some of the most fabulous people-watching in Marrakech. As a bonus, it also has one of the friendliest maître d's in town – do say *bonjour* to monsieur Moustakidis.

The sweeping central staircase and chequered tiles recall the building's 1920s origins, though design firm Studio KO has given the space a modern update. Come for French classics such as onion soup and beef tartare, served with a reliable wine list of both local and French producers. Complimentary bites are offered from 18.00 for those enjoying an aperitivo.
Corner of Boulevard El Mansour Eddahbi and Avenue Imam Malik
+212 (0)5 2443 3038
grandcafedelaposte.restaurant

Must-try
Date milkshake from Café Clock, Kasbah
Need to fuel up before an afternoon of haggling in the souks? Blending Moroccan dates and homemade vanilla ice cream, Café Clock's delicious milkshake will provide you with an intense hit of energy and local flavour.
cafeclock.com

6

Nomad, Medina
Hot ticket

It's arguable which is the biggest drawcard of this restaurant housed in a former carpet shop: the tasty new-Moroccan cuisine or its rooftop terrace overlooking the colourful spice square, Place Rahba Lakdima.

Kick things off with the fish balls in spicy tomato-based sauce, or Tunisian *brik* (a deep-fried pastry). The lack of alcohol doesn't deter the crowds; reservations are recommended, and in peak season essential. If you can't snag a rooftop table, the indoor options are also top-drawer – after all, the design was handled by Swiss interior designer Romain Michel Menière – and a tad more comfortable in summer.
1 Derb Aarjane
+212 (0)5 2438 1609
nomadmarrakech.com

7

Ksar Essaoussane, Medina
Generous serving

With its fountain, colourful tiles and hidden staircases that lead to the dining rooms above, it's worth booking a table at this Saadian-era mansion for the decor alone. Dinner starts with a rose-water handwash before guests are served a fixed menu fit for a king: salads, tagines and desserts aplenty. A half-bottle of wine is also included.
3 Rue des Ksour, Derb El Messoudyenne
+212 (0)5 2444 0632
essaoussane.com

Three hotel restaurants

01 La Table du Riad at Riad 72, Medina: Owner Giovanna Cinel's approach is very much farm-to-table. When in season, don't miss the *berkoukech* (hand-rolled Moroccan pasta) topped with grilled octopus and sautéed vegetables. The courtyard patio has a winsome evening ambiance, while the rooftop offers excellent views.
riad72.com

02 Assyl at Selman Marrakech, Chrifia: Assyl serves some of the finest cuisine in Marrakech in an exotic Ottoman-inspired setting (the stables, designed by Jacques Garcia, are home to Arabian horses that entertain diners during Sunday brunch at sister restaurant Le Pavillon). For a true taste of this country, start with the range of Moroccan salads that combine unexpected flavours, followed by a rabbit tagine with confit of onions, raisins and almonds.
selman-marrakech.com

03 La Grande Table Marocaine at Royal Mansour, Medina: This restaurant has few peers when it comes to elegance and grandeur. Chef Yannick Alléno has created a menu heavy on classics such as seafood *pastilla* (a filo-pastry dish) and seven-vegetable couscous. Adding to the charm is the music provided by traditional oud (short-neck lute) players.
royalmansour.com

9

El Fenn, Medina
Table with a view

Seasonal dishes, a bohemian vibe and first-class views of Mosquée Koutoubia make this rooftop hotel (*see page 15*) restaurant a favourite lunchtime spot. The menu by head chef Fouad Ajili changes daily but you can expect a meat or fish dish alongside fresh salads made with organic fruits and vegetables from the Ourika Valley.

Lunch is served from 12.00 to 14.30 sharp and there are two dinner seatings. Time your reservation to coincide with sunset, settle into one of the oversized banquettes with a bottle of rosé and you're in for a rather special evening.
*2 Derb Moulay Abdullah
Ben Hezzian
+212 (0)5 2444 1210
el-fenn.com*

8

Le Trou au Mur, Medina
Genuine taste

The menu here is unusual in that it presents family recipes that normally wouldn't be tasted outside the home. But owner James Wix realised that these are the authentic flavours of Morocco, regardless of whether they're thought to be suitable for a restaurant.

Opt for *tride* (pancakes with saffron sauce, lentils and chicken) or *bourkoukech*. Whatever you choose, we'd recommend skipping the British dishes on the menu – after all, we're in Marrakech.
*39 Derb El Farnatchi,
Rue Souk El Fassis
+212 (0)5 2438 4900
letrouaumur.com*

10

I Limoni, Medina
Hidden surprise

Behind a modest door in a quiet part of the medina, I Limoni serves Italian home-style cooking in a pretty orange-tree-filled courtyard. Owner Adriano Pirani, an architect from Bologna, likes to keep the menu simple yet tasty: think antipasti, homemade pastas and good-to-the-last-bite tiramisu. Sadly, since the venue doesn't have an alcohol license, the ragu will have to be enjoyed without a bottle of chianti.
40 Dyour Saboun
+212 (0)5 2438 3030

11

Bagatelle, Gueliz
Gallic heritage

Bagatelle has been in business since 1949, when Morocco was still a French protectorate and current owner Serge Blanc-Collomb's grandmother was in the kitchen. Then as now, the restaurant was known for its brasserie cuisine: think steak frites, escargots and terrine. A daily oyster delivery is paramount as Blanc-Collomb's patrons get through at least 100 a day. Family photos and those from Gueliz's bygone days decorate the walls, while a stained-glass ceiling crowns the art deco bar.
103 Rue Yougoslavie
+212 (0)5 2443 0274
bagatelle-marrakech.com

⑫

Plus61, Gueliz
Modern Aussie

As the name suggests (hint: it's a dialing code) this hotspot serves Australian fare, which co-owner Cassandra Karinsky – founder of interiors brand Kulchi (*see page 55*) – describes as "clean, modern" and tempered "with flavours from the Mediterranean and Asia." Karinsky opened Plus61 together with head chef Andrew Cibej and Sebastian de Gzell, co-owner of Nomad (*see page 30*).

The menu is not the sort that's obsessed with microscopic vegetables and ceremonious mousses. Instead expect gyoza dumplings, homemade ricotta and fried cuttlefish with sweet chilli. Breads, pasta, cheese and yoghurts are made in-house each day. Plus, Karinsky's love of a good cocktail ensures that those served here are the very best you'll find in town.

96 Rue Mohammed El Beqal
+212 (0)5 2420 7020
plus61.com

13

Dar Rhizlane, Hivernage
Reimagined Moroccan

Most visitors head to Hivernage for the wild nightlife but a candlelit dinner served under orange trees and bougainvilleas in the courtyard at Dar Rhizlane is reason enough for us. The menu may be traditional but mains such as sea-bream tagine explore more adventurous flavours than your typical Marrakshi restaurant. Manager Martine Gaertner calls it "revisited Moroccan cuisine". The sweetened carrots appetiser is a must.
Avenue Jnane El Harti
+212 (0)5 2442 1303
dar-rhizlane.com

14

Le Petit Cornichon, Gueliz
Good value

Erwann Lance's (*pictured*) sleek bistro offers a fixed-price lunch of French fare that's beloved for its value as much as its taste. Created by chef Manaf el Bloul, the menu changes seasonally but always includes the popular dishes of ceviche and carpaccio.

The punchy blue-and-yellow interior, designed by Selma Laraqui of Aqsel, references the bold palette of the nearby Jardin Majorelle (*see page 80*). In the evenings the lights dim and it becomes a more formal affair with à la carte dining.
Rue Moulay Ali
+212 (0)5 2442 1251
lepetitcornichon.ma

15

Naranj, Medina
Modern Lebanese

Husband-and-wife team Wahib Kalai and Ruba Mawas have spiced up the local food scene with a little Levantine flair. He's of Syrian origin and she's Lebanese, so the cuisine they serve includes dishes such as smoky baba ghanoush, *fatet batinjane* (aubergine, ground beef, tomatoes and yoghurt on grilled pita) and slow-cooked lamb with bulgur. For dessert, we recommend the halva mousse. There's no alcohol licence but the fresh juices and lemonades make up for it.
84 Rue Riad Zitoun El Jdid
+212 (0)5 2438 6805
naranj.ma

Lunch
Daytime dining

❶ La Famille, Medina
Heightened vegetables

There are limited vegetarian options available in the medina so meat-free La Famille (open for lunch only) fills a much-needed gap. The dessert counter, which you'll get a good look at when entering, is also popular and filled with fruit tarts and chocolate cakes.

Diners sit at long communal tables in an airy space with rattan accents and white-washed walls; those quick enough may snag a perch in the rambling garden. The only downside is that La Famille has become a victim of its own success, and the laid-back atmosphere it was originally known for sometimes gets lost in the hustle. On which note, reservations are mandatory.
34 Derb Jdid
+212 (0)5 2438 5295

❷ Amal, Gueliz
Dining for a cause

Amal equips disadvantaged women with culinary and service skills so they can go on to have careers in the hospitality industry. But don't think this is an amateur operation – the cooking and service give top restaurants a run for their money.

The menu is classic Moroccan, with a handful of internationally inspired options. On Fridays, the traditional day for eating couscous, the centre is choc-a-bloc and bookings are essential.
Corner of Rue Allal Ben Ahmed and Rue Ibn Sina
+212 (0)5 2444 6896
amalnonprofit.org

4

BlackChich, Medina
Southern flavour

Housed in the remains
of the city's first church,
BlackChich serves a menu
that it describes as "forgotten
Berber recipes and a taste
of Senegal". Special dishes
include chicken *rfissa* (lentils
and chicken in butter sauce)
and *seffa* (vermicelli with
sweet almonds), recipes that
co-owner Kudo Fakhredine
recalls from his upbringing in
southern Morocco. Note: the
venue is not to be confused
with sister venue Bakchich,
a diner on the same street.
*1 Derb Nakouss Riad Zitoune
El Jdid
+212 (0)6 5485 0600*

3

Shtatto, Medina
Hip hangout

This rooftop café in the
heart of the medina attracts
a fashion-forward crowd
as some of the city's finest
designers have their studios
on the floors below. Classic
lunchtime fare – think tagines
and fresh juices – is prepared
in the small open kitchen and
served in a bright-and-breezy
setting decorated with bamboo
plants and green banquettes.

The views are fabulous
but best enjoyed around sunset
in the summer, as the terrace
can become something of
a suntrap. Check Shtatto's
social media pages for Sunday
afternoon events where local
DJs take to the decks and the
rooftop becomes a dance floor.
*81 Derb Nkhal
+212 (0)5 2437 5538*

Must-try
Tanjia from Chez Lamine
Hadj Mustapha, Medina
Hadj Lamine is renowned
for having served the royal
family. Alongside *mechoui*
(spit-roasted lamb), the house
speciality is *tanjia* (a rich,
meaty stew cooked in clay
pots). It's a staple of the
Moroccan food scene for
a good reason.
18-26 Souk Ablouh

Tea and coffee
Pick me up

1

Café des Épices, Medina
Vantage point

The sister venue to Nomad (*see page 30*) offers breakfast, lunch and dinner – but, above all, we'd recommend dropping by for a hot drink. If you're after something stronger than a mint tea opt for a *nouss nouss* (half coffee, half milk), served with the obligatory Moroccan patisserie.

Rooftop guests are afforded great views of the spice square, Rahba Lakdima (hence the name), while the first-floor gallery is better suited to those craving some peace and quiet.
75 Derb Rahba Lakdima
+212 (0)5 2439 1770
cafedesepices.ma

2

Amandine, Gueliz
Sweet eats

For those in the know, this patisserie – one of the first of its kind in Marrakech – is the go-to for baked goods of both Moroccan and French persuasion. Begin your exploration with a *corne de gazelle* (an almond-and-orange-blossom-filled curl of pastry). The colourful macarons are another favourite.

The adjoining café has plentiful seating where you can enjoy your purchases, along with some music and a genteel atmosphere.
177 Rue Mohammed El Beqal
+212 (0)5 2444 9612
amandinemarrakech.com

Mint tea
—
Somewhat misleadingly, Marrakshis refer to mint tea as "Berber whisky". It's prepared with a green-tea base and a heaping of sugar, then poured from up high into a tea cup to achieve a foam. It's a mark of hospitality; you might be offered it when shopping in the souks.

 3

ChiChaoua Tea Room, Medina
Simple tea service

It's easy to miss this old-town tea room, which is identified by a small, eye-level sign painted on a door on Rahba Lakdima. Tip: it's right next to Café des Épices (*see opposite*), which is also owned by dynamic hospitality mover-and-shaker Kamal Laftimi.

Mint-green walls, a bold pink sofa, geometric tiles by local artisans and a vinyl player round out the minimal-yet-cheery decor. A small but excellent, and at times adventurous, selection of teas are on offer – perfectly accompanied by the cakes of the day, which are walked over from sister restaurant Nomad (*see page 30*).
Rahba Lakdima
+212 (0)5 2433 8470

Must-try
Sfenj, citywide
These sugary doughnuts are cooked on the spot in stalls or by itinerant cart-holders all around Marrakech. If purchasing from the former, ask for a cup of mint tea to pair with the chewy goodness. For extra crispiness, make like a local and request your doughnut be smashed and returned for a second fry.

Out-of-town dining
Worth the journey

❶

Kasbah Tamadot, Asni
Scenic setting

This restaurant is part of a spectacular hotel in the foothills of the Atlas Mountains that was bought by Sir Richard Branson on one of his round-the-world ballooning trips. Head chef Yassine Khalal honed his craft at the Royal Mansour (*see page 16*) and here makes the most of what's grown in the on-site vegetable garden, including 23 varieties of tomatoes. Bread is baked each day in a traditional Berber clay oven. To work up an appetite, embark on a pre-lunch hike in the valley.
BP 67, Asni
+212 (0)5 2436 8200
virginlimitededition.com/kasbah-tamadot

❷

Le Flouka, Lalla Takerkoust
Settle in

Heading out of town for Sunday lunch is a rite for Marrakshis, and you needn't go far to find a new landscape, a cool breeze and excellent fare. We suggest arriving at this hotel-restaurant around midday for a swim (included with the price of lunch) or a pre-meal drink at the bar.

The restaurant, which overlooks a pretty lake, excels in grilled dishes such as tomahawk steaks and *gambas à la plancha* (prawns). By about 16.00, as the crowd orders a third round of rosé, we suspect you'll be tempted to extend your stay.
BP 45, Barrage Lalla Takerkoust
+212 (0)6 6449 2660
leflouka-marrakech.com

Who knew it would be so hot in the desert?

❸
Scarabeo Camp, Agafay Desert
Desert dining

Within an hour's drive of
Marrakech is a rocky, lunar-
like desert landscape called
the Agafay. A host of luxury,
camp-like hotels have popped
up within it in recent years,
chief among them Scarabeo
Camp (*see page 24*). Its on-site
restaurant is open to the public
for lunch and dinner and will
even send a Jeep to pick you
up from town.

A feast of salads, tagines
and wine is served among
the rustic charm of the
Bedouin tents. If it's lunchtime,
do linger after your meal in the
library; dinner guests should
enjoy a post-meal refreshment
by the campfire while gazing
at the Milky Way.
Agafay Desert
+212 (0)5 2420 1117
scarabeocamp.com

1 4

5 6

7   8

9

1 — 4 Chez Hassan Sbaai 34: You'll know when you've reached Hassan Sbaai's barbecue stall in the Jemaa El Fna market: just look for the smoke billowing from the hot plates filled with spicy merguez sausages. Order a plate of these, some fresh tomatoes and stuff it all into a *khobz* (bread roll) to create a sandwich as the locals do.
Jemaa El Fna

5 — 6 Pâtisserie Nawal: Arrive at about 17.00 when the staff start serving *msemen* (pancake-like bread) stuffed with harissa, onion, olives and cheese. Pair it with a cup of mint tea and you're halfway to being Marrakshi.
Rue Koutoubia

7 — 9 31: Carb-heavy *maakouda* (potato cakes) are lightly spiced and fried. You'll find them offered with harissa sauce at stall 31. Often an appetizer, some like to stuff them inside a loaf of bread for a sandwich on the go.
Jemaa El Fna

10 — 11 Krita 14: This stall on the edge of Jemaa El Fna, also known as 14, opens only when it has fresh seafood – so there's no schedule. The calamari here is lightly battered, fried and best scooped up with fresh tomato sauce and *zaalouk* (tomato-and-aubergine dip).
Jemaa El Fna

10   11

Drinks
Where to imbibe

②
Baromètre, Gueliz
Basement blends

Brothers Hamza and Soufiane Hadni returned from Europe to create this cocktail bar with the spirt of a speakeasy but all the trimmings of a modern-day watering hole (including comfortable seating). And it's not hard to find: just look for the giant metal "B".

Highlights include the Rosé du Matin (a potent mix of gin, rosé, vodka, red berries and rose water), or you can keep the memories of the souks alive with a Marrakech Market, made with whisky, cinnamon, saffron syrup and orange.
Rue Moulay Ali
+212 (0)6 6688 6798

①
Terrasse des Épices, Medina
Drink up

Terrasse des Épices is one of the few haunts in the medina that serves alcohol, making its rooftop terrace popular come time for a sundowner. Enjoy the view with a bottle of rosé, the drink of choice for a warm Marrakshi afternoon, or a refreshing glass of Casablanca beer on draft.

Grab one of the pagoda-type tables if you're staying for dinner, although do keep in mind that evenings can be cold and the terrace here is rather unprotected.
15 Souk Cherifia, Sidi Abdelaziz
+212 (0)5 2437 5904
terrassedesepices.com

❸ L'Italien, Medina
Opulent watering hole

The legendary La Mamounia (*see page 17*) is said to have been a favourite of Sir Winston Churchill – and perhaps its five bars had something to do with it. The splendid L'Italien is easily identified by its red-velvet seats.

The live music in the evening is always entertaining, as is observing the glamorous clientele. There isn't a bad time to stop by: the mood is perpetually lively. But do freshen up for your visit – the hotel, as in days of yore, insists on a smart dress code.
Avenue Bab Jdid
+212 (0)5 2438 8600
mamounia.com

❹ Le 68, Gueliz
French charm

The space may be cramped, and the smoking area at the entrance only adds to this effect, but that doesn't stop a fashionable crowd from gathering here for post-work drinks. The wine list is carefully curated with options from both Morocco and overseas, and paired well with charcuterie and cheese boards.

Head upstairs for comforting French dishes such as Saint Jacques-style oyster gratin and raclette. Portions are generous and service is friendly.
68 Rue de la Liberté
+212 (0)5 2444 9742
le-68-bar-a-vin-marrakech-restaurant.business.site

Pick of the bunch

It's often a surprise to visitors that this north African kingdom produces wine. While the industry reached its peak during the French protectorate period from 1912 to 1956, it's been experiencing a revival in recent years thanks to foreign investment. Below you'll find our rundown of the best bottles. You're unlikely to see them back at home – few are exported – so dive in and enjoy them while you can.

01 **Volubilia rosé by Domaine de la Zouina:** Produced using predominantly syrah grapes, this light rosé has flavours of red fruits and a hint of spice. It's perfect to pair with a tagine but also a top choice for an afternoon by the pool.

02 **Perle gris by Domaine du Val d'Argan:** This organic "grey wine" from Frenchman Charles Melia's Essaouira winery has hints of peach and citrus. Best served chilled as an aperitif.

03 **Éclipse blanc by Les Deux Domaines:** The full-bodied éclipse white is produced near Meknes and made from marsanne, roussanne and viognier grapes. This tipple makes a good pairing with a lemon-chicken tagine.

04 **S de Siroua syrah by Domaine Ouled Thaleb:** Produced by Morocco's oldest winery, Domaine des Ouled Thaleb, this red is smooth and silky with a smoky tinge, and made entirely from syrah grapes. It goes well with beef *tanjia* and *mechoui*.

Retail
—— Gaining
purchase

Since the 11th century camel-loads of goods – rugs, textiles, leather and more – have flowed out of the markets of Marrakech and into every corner of the world. It's a city brimming with creativity thanks to the many artisans who call it home.

There's also a rising pool of talented young designers – homegrown and expats alike – who are setting up fashion labels, ceramic studios, weaving mills and other ventures. The retail scene is enriched through their efforts and melds contemporary design with the country's traditional handicraft practices.

Of course, no visit would be complete without a whirl around the souks – the medina's vast markets which are filled with inconceivable quantities of both treasure and tat. It takes some skill to discern which is which, and then there's the haggling itself – we hope you've been practising.

1

Marrakshi Life, Hay Al Masar
Market leader

This is arguably Morocco's definitive fashion label. The brand, started in 2013 by New York photographer Randall Bachner (*pictured*), has a unique look that brings to mind the draping, luxurious outfits of Ottoman sultans, plus a hint of wide-fitting French Riviera chic. And despite the rather specific aesthetic, there's plenty to suit every wardrobe, from straight-and-narrow (think classic jackets and striped shirts) to avant garde: a canary-yellow jumpsuit, anyone?

In Bachner's studio-shop visitors can see the clothing being made on traditional Moroccan looms. If there's a fashion equivalent of farm-to-table dining, this is it.
933 Route de Safi
+212 (0)5 2508 5267
marrakshilife.com

Charming, isn't he?

②
Laly, Medina
Material worth

What sets a Laly item apart
is its material. Owner and
designer Badra Bengeloune
sources fabrics from Paris
and elsewhere in Europe
(often from the same suppliers
as luxury brands such as
Hermès) to create elegant
womenswear that, while
minimal in design, has a
playful Moroccan touch.

"I pay great attention to
making clothes as comfortable
as possible – that are easy to
wear again and again," says
Bengeloune, who has a list of
high-profile clients. Laly has
two outposts: this one, which
opened in February 2019, and
another to the northwest of
the medina.
104 Hay Elkennaria Essoucha
+212 (0)5 2509 5650

③
Hanout, Medina
Old meets new

"I grew up in a family with a
great tradition of dressmaking,
embroidery and knitting –
during the summer holiday,
that was how I made money,"
says Meriem Rawlings, the
Moroccan owner-designer
of Hanout. Today Rawlings
creates maxi dresses, jumpsuits
and silk kaftans from colourful
fabrics sourced from Morocco
and India, as well as leather
jackets and accessories that
she embroiders with one-off
Berber jewellery from the
Atlas Mountains.

This shop (the other is in
Riad Zitoun) is petite but packs
a punch. It also has quite the
client list, including members
of Morocco's royal family.
194 Rue Mouassine
+212 (0)5 2437 8736
hanoutboutique.com

4

Norya Ayron, Medina
One-off pieces

Algerian designer Norya Ayron
(*pictured*) is the undisputed
doyenne of women's fashion
in Morocco. A number of big
names have worn her designs:
Kate Moss, Juliette Binoche
and Sharon Stone, to name
a few. Originally an events
organiser, Ayron shifted her
attention to fashion in 2013.

Each piece she designs
is a one-off. So while the
showroom may look replete
with luxuriously patterned
dresses, you can be sure there's
no stock room – once it's gone,
it's gone. Everything is made
in Ayron's atelier in Marrakech
with Portuguese fabrics that are
exclusive to the label. The shop
sits above Le Jardin Marrakech
(*see page 26*).
32 Souk Jeld
+212 (0)6 6129 5990
norya-ayron.com

One-stop shop
——
Though 33 Rue Majorelle lacks
a clothing range of its own,
it stocks many of the brands
featured in our retail rundown,
including Laly (*see opposite*)
and Le Chapelier (*see page
135*). A good place to go,
then, if you're tight on time.
33ruemajorelle.com

6
Max & Jan, Medina
Mixed bag

The multi-brand shop Max & Jan occupies a 300-year-old building in the medina, spanning a huge fashion section, accessories and homeware and even a terrace restaurant and café. It's an inviting set-up – the likes of which is unusual in Marrakech.

The heart of the collection is the in-house line of womenswear designed by Swiss and Belgian co-owners Maximilian Scharl and Jan Pauwels. You'll also find perfume by Héritage Berbère, glassware and ceramics from local artisans, and much more besides. Once you're done browsing, pop upstairs for a juice or a coffee.
14 Rue Amsefah
+212 (0)5 2433 6406
maxandjan.com

❺
Akbar Delights, Medina
Globetrotting designs

This little shop is stowed away in a space behind Jemaa El Fna. It's an explosion of colour: cushions, kaftans, *babouches* (Moroccan slippers), scarves – you name it, you'll find it.

The style is more ornate and overtly Moorish than most other fashion brands in town. "The main idea is to revisit traditional embroideries and create, say, jackets or coats that you buy in Marrakech but wear perfectly well in Europe or America," says Isabelle Dobry, one of three French co-owners who set up the brand in 2004.

There's another Akbar Delights outpost, plus sister label Moor (with a greater focus on homeware), in Gueliz.
Place Bab Fteuh
+212 (0)6 7166 1307
akbardelightscollections.com

New wardrobe, tick!

More fashion brands

01 **Kitan, Medina:** A colourful, small-batch womenswear label by Japanese designer Mai Yamazaki. You'll find her shop across the road from Malakut (*see page 54*), while the atelier is just a few doors down.
11 Derb Smara Kandil

02 **Maison ARTC, Gueliz:** An avant garde label whose eccentric designs are inspired by traditional Arab and Berber clothing – boosted by kitsch patterns and bright colours, that is.
maisonartc.com

03 **Topolina, Sidi Ghanem:** An intensely bright, bold label by Isabelle Topolina, who has been lauded by fashion titans such as *Vogue*. Her men's and womenswear designs thrive on strong patterns and bring to mind the grand, ceremonial outfits of India, Japan and the Middle East.
topolina.shop

Homeware
Living design

 1

36 Mouassine, Medina
Ceramics and more

French-Moroccan designer Corinne Bensimon is well-known in Marrakech for her ceramics line, which, until this shop's opening in 2019, was only available from the Beldi Country Club (*see pages 84 to 85*). Now visitors to the Red City can browse her full line of wares within a stone's throw of Jemaa El Fna. Bensimon has also stocked the three-storey space with hats by Le Chapelier, wooden cutlery by Moroccan-Japanese label Michi, vintage glassware and more.
36 Rue Mouassine
+212 0(6) 7548 0102

Treasure trove

Designers Alessandra Lippini and Fabrizio Bizzari's Ministero del Gusto is a funky building of Lippini's own creation. Inside you'll find one-off pieces of furniture (also hers) and vintage clothing such as 1920s Chanel. By appointment only.
ministerodelgusto.com

3

V Barkowski, Medina
Lots of linen

The linen pieces designed by Valérie Barkowski – owner of Dar Kawa (*see pages 20 to 21*) – are an omnipresent motif in the homes of Marrakech's high society; everyone wants to furnish their tables, bathrooms and beds with the French designer's creations.

In this cavernous shop next to Mustapha Blaoui (*see page 54*) you'll find placemats, napkins, towels and bed linen, plus smooth-as-silk *babouches* and a small line of leather goods (a relatively recent addition to the brand's remit). Everything is made in Morocco and stands as testament to the high level of craftsmanship in the country.
Dar Bacha, 142 Arset Aouzal
+212 (0)6 2449 4001
valeriebarkowski.com

2

LRNCE, Sidi Ghanem
Worth the journey

The industrial neighbourhood of Sidi Ghanem may not be the most attractive destination but a visit to this studio and shop will make it worthwhile. Belgian designer Laurence Leenaert (*pictured*) moved here with her nascent label in 2015 after quitting Ghent's Royal Academy of Fine Arts.

Her pieces are instantly recognisable by their colourful and playful yet minimal design. Leenaert started with bags but has since expanded into carpets, pillows, sandals, ceramics and mirrors too. Everything is handmade in Morocco by some 35 artisans. Be sure to check the website for opening hours.
59 Sidi Ghanem
+212 (0)5 2420 0108
lrnce.com

Specialist retail
Out of the ordinary

1

6 Souk Jeld, Medina
Nostalgic melodies

In endearing Moroccan fashion, this record store doesn't even have a name. But you can't miss it: just head towards Souk Jeld – near Terrasse des Épices (*see page 44*) and look and listen out for two old foxes blasting Moroccan rock on their vinyl player. The shop is a trip through the 1970s; there are no price tags, so you'll have to haggle.
6 Souk Jeld
+212 (0)6 7128 2128

2

Malakut, Medina
Eye for design

Though Salah-eddine Bouhiri makes his living as a mathematics professor, his real calling is as a ceramicist and designer. You'll often find him at his pint-sized shop, which sells ceramics (*see pages 134 to 135*) with undulating shapes and minimal designs, as well as scarves made by women artisans from southern Morocco.
54 Triq Sidi Abd El Aziz
+212 (0)6 4205 6028

Fixed-price haven

A household name in the retail scene, Mustapha Blaoui is nothing short of an Aladdin's cave of lamps, rugs, ceramics and other typical Moroccan homeware. It's also the more tourist-friendly of the traditional shops, if bartering isn't for you.
144 Rue Bab Doukkala

❶
Kulchi, Medina
Bespoke service

Cassandra Karinsky made the move to Marrakech in 2005 but didn't found Kulchi (which means "everything" in Arabic) for another five years. While working for magazines such as *Marie Claire Maison*, the Aussie often had to source rugs for shoots and soon developed a deep knowledge of, and passion for, the craft. "It was all very fascinating to me," she says. "There's so much beauty and history in each piece."

Kulchi produces its own collection in collaboration with rug shop Bazar du Sud, with which Karinsky shares a space in the medina, and stocks vintage numbers too. Unlike other rug shops, service is personalised: Karinsky helps customers pick out the perfect rug or organises to have one made specially, whether it's for the home, an office or a magazine shoot. "It can be a big investment so it's important for us to make sure our clients are happy with their final purchase, a piece they will live with for many years," she says.
60 Rahba Lakdima
+212 (0)6 3922 1259
kulchi.com

❸
Magasin Général, Sidi Ghanem
European collectibles

This warehouse-like shop is a trove of reconditioned vintage furniture, art, glassware and general miscellanea – think typewriters, travel trunks and gymnastics sets – from fin de siècle, 1920s and 1930s France, Belgium and England. Belgian owner Délphine Mottet, who used to run a riad in the medina, regularly travels back to Europe to source items but also has agents on the ground. "I use my mother," she says. "She's in Belgium and goes to the markets every Sunday."

All the wares have been faithfully restored and at times adapted for modernity's sake; furniture is reupholstered here using Belgian fabrics.
369 Sidi Ghanem
+212 (0)5 2433 6673
magasin-general-marrakech.com

2
Soufiane Zarib, Medina
Tasteful designs

Soufiane Zarib (*pictured, on right*) is a third-generation Marrakshi and arguably one of the country's top designers. His eponymous label's speciality is Berber rugs, made in Middle Atlas from sheep and goat wool. The styles are contemporary, pared-down and often boast colours that you wouldn't see in more traditional shops.

Zarib's flagship also stocks vintage Moroccan homeware, as well as a small in-house furniture range and its own line of linen jumpsuits. Once you've signed for all your purchases, pop upstairs to the rooftop restaurant, Coles, for lunch.
16 Rue Riad Laarous
+212 (0)6 1528 5690
soufiane-zarib.com

❸

Les Nomades de Marrakech,
Medina
Family affair

Spread across a 600-year-old
building, this family-run rug
emporium is overseen by
fifth-generation owner Namous
Abderrahim (*pictured*). It's
home to some 22,000 rugs of
every size and style imaginable.

While there are plenty
of Arabic-style carpets
here (recognisable by their
colourful, geometric patterns),
the main attraction are the
more free-spirited, simple
Berber variants – the unique
patterns of which are designed
by craftsmen in moments of
inspiration. This is also the
best spot for sourcing a vintage
rug, whether you're after
something from the 1880s
or the 1980s.
40 Zaouiat Lahdar
+212 (0)5 2438 1845
lesnomadesdemarrakech.com

Souks
Market trade

Where to start
──

There's nothing like sifting through the souks to find a treasure. It can feel a bit overwhelming but don't worry, we've created a rundown of which ones to hit whether you're after hand-dyed textiles, *babouches* or a vintage tea set (*see page 137*).

Culture
—— Stealing
the scene

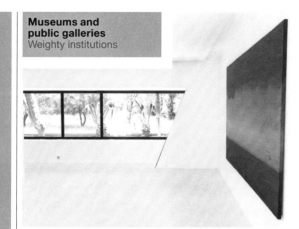

Morocco has long been a magnet for artists who have drawn inspiration from its multifarious landscapes, hazy light and artistic heritage. And yet, it's only since the mid-2000s that African art – especially that created in the past century – has begun to receive the recognition it deserves.

Since the 1950s a clutch of commercial galleries has opened in the city, particularly in the modern neighbourhood of Gueliz. Together with the advent of world-class museums such as the Musée Yves Saint Laurent and Macaal, and the arrival of 1-54 Contemporary African Art Fair on home soil, these have shifted the focus of the art market from Casablanca and Rabat to Marrakech.

Of course, the higgledy-piggledy medina is also home to a range of artistic ventures, including one or two foundations promoting Moroccan culture through diverse exhibitions and events. Sadly the live-music scene here leaves a lot to be desired – rather than smooth jazz, think cabaret and neon lights. So skip that and get your cultural fix from the visual-arts offering instead.

①

Macaal, Annakhil
Creative mission

The Musée d'Art Contemporain Africain Al Maaden (Macaal) has been shaking up the art scene since it was founded in 2016 by property magnate Alami Lazraq and his son Othman (*see page 124*). The ethos: this is a private museum with a very public vision. Macaal is dedicated to bringing contemporary African art to a broader audience through rotating exhibitions of its ever-growing collection, which the family began amassing some 40 years ago, and a diverse education programme.

Designed by French architect Didier Lefort, the geometric building is an architectural feat with a naturally lit interior and a sculpture garden that doubles as a cinema. Macaal is an extension of the family's not-for-profit association Fondation Alliances, which supports cultural development in Morocco.
Al Maaden, Sidi Youssef, Ben Ali
+ 212 (0)6 7692 4492
macaal.org

Art to the fore
———

Next door to Macaal is the Parc de Sculptures Al Maaden, another initiative by Fondation Alliances. Peppered throughout the golf course are site-specific, large-scale sculptures made by artists who hail from Morocco, China, India, Argentina and more.
almaaden.golf

②

Musée Mathaf Farid Belkahia, Annakhil
Artistic legacy

If you plan to visit the Musée de la Palmeraie (*see page 81*) – which is worth it for the jaw-dropping cactus garden alone – be sure to pop into this museum devoted to the late Moroccan artist Farid Belkahia. A taxi from the city centre takes roughly 20 minutes.

Belkahia was born into a bourgeois family in Marrakech and grew up surrounded by art and those who create it. He went on to study at various academies in Europe and became one of Morocco's most distinguished modern artists.

On permanent display at Musée Mathaf Farid Belkahia – housed within the studio where the artist worked for almost 30 years – is a vast selection of his works, from paintings and metalwork to naturally dyed leather.
Dar Tounsi, BP 649 Marrakech Principale, Palmeraie Nord
+ 212 (0)5 2432 8959
fondationfaridbelkahia.com

❸

Musée de Mouassine, Medina
Original home

This museum may be dedicated to the arts of Morocco but it's also architecturally intriguing, located in a traditional residence built in the 17th century and originally split into two parts (public and private). Painstakingly restored between 2012 and 2014, the awe-inspiring structure retains many of its original elements, including multi-coloured tiled floors, intricately carved wooden doors and pink plaster walls in the central courtyard.

The museum is inextricably linked to the painter Abdelhay Mellakh, who was born in the house in 1947 and whose studio remains intact. Exhibitions have focused on themes such as decorative art and 16th-century architecture, while musical evenings take place from October to May.
4-5 Derb El Hammam,
Rue Mouassine
+212 (0)5 2438 5721
museedemouassine.com

4

Macma, Gueliz
Passion project

Founded in 2016 by art collector Nabil El Mallouki, the Musée d'Art et de Culture de Marrakech (Macma) was built upon a collection of Moroccan artefacts and orientalist paintings. El Mallouki worked in banking before leaving his job and founding the nearby Matisse Art Gallery (*see page 66*) in 1999. "The bank was my job; art is my passion," he says. In 2018 he established The Orientalist Museum too.

Alongside a permanent collection, Macma hosts temporary exhibitions that celebrate subjects including the history of Moroccan photography and film posters.
Passage Ghandouri,
61 Rue Yougoslavie
+212 (0)7 0024 2572
museemacma.com

5

Maison de la Photographie, Medina
House of cards

Opened by Hamid Mergani and Patrick Manac'h in 2009, Maison de la Photographie presents some 10,000 photographs taken between 1870 and 1960. Highlights include a series of 1960s postcards showcasing typical scenes in Marrakech, while Daniel Chicault's documentary colour photographs and a rare set of 800 glass plates capture the wild landscape of the High Atlas and their Berber residents.

Exhibitions have explored everything from palm groves to Moroccan women. Draw back the curtains that conceal the doorways to each room – like an old-school photographer dipping beneath a hood – and be sure to pick up a couple of prints and postcards before you leave.
46 Rue Souk Ahal Fassi
+212 (0)5 2438 5721
maisondelaphotographie.ma

6
Musée Berbère, Majorelle
Traditional beauty

Tucked away in the lush oasis of the Jardin Majorelle (*see page 80*), the Musée Berbère shines a spotlight on Berber art and culture. Yves Saint Laurent's business partner and great love of 50 years, Pierre Bergé, founded the museum in 2011, six years before he established the nearby Musée Yves Saint Laurent (*see right*).

The permanent exhibition features more than 600 objects, from the 18th century to the 1960s, that provide a window onto the north African indigenous tribes found between the Rif and the Sahara. Traditional craftsmanship skills are on display in everyday and ceremonial artefacts, while the rituals of the Berbers are expressed through festive costumes. A highlight is the mirrored room of jewels: the starry ceiling adds to the sense of bedazzlement as you admire silver necklaces and wrist cuffs studded with amber and coral.
Rue Yves Saint Laurent
+212 (0)5 2429 8686
jardinmajorelle.com

7
Musée Yves Saint Laurent, Majorelle
House design

Though Yves Saint Laurent was steeped in the exquisite world of Parisian haute couture, he spent much of his time in Morocco. "While Paris is about creation, this is about emotion and inspiration," says Björn Dahlström, the Casablanca-born director of the Musée Yves Saint Laurent. "It was here he discovered colour: the pinks, reds and oranges he was known for."

This hugely popular museum was designed by Paris-based architecture firm Studio KO (*see pages 72 to 73*) and opened in 2017. The black interior of the permanent exhibit is lined with documents and photographs from the designer's life, as well as projections of catwalk models marching like newly shod ponies showing off his creations.
Rue Yves Saint Laurent
+212 (0)5 2429 8686
museeyslmarrakech.com

Commercial galleries
Trading places

Galerie 127, Gueliz
Talent incubator

It's easy to miss Nathalie Locatelli's photography gallery, located on the second floor of a mixed-purpose building on Avenue Mohammed V. Erected in 1922, the art deco complex was originally divided into apartments and is now also home to various medical practices. "Yes, it's an unusual mix," she says with a smile.

Locatelli founded Gallery 127 in 2006 and, to this day, it's the only gallery dedicated to photography in Morocco. "There still isn't a great demand for photography in Africa and it's my aim to change that," says Locatelli. Her approach centres around forging relationships with artists at the outset of their careers and sticking with them as their style develops – she's been with some for more than a decade. "It's a real passion."
2F, 127 Avenue Mohammed V
+212 (0)5 2443 2667
galerie127.com

Comptoir des Mines Galerie, Gueliz
Artistic residence

This peach-coloured art gallery is the most recent offering from Hicham Daoudi, president of Art Holding Morocco, who started out in agriculture before trading crops for canvases. In 2002 he established CMOOA (an auction house in Casablanca) and in 2009 launched Diptyk (*see page 71*), Morocco's first contemporary-art magazine. He went on to found Comptoir des Mines Galerie in 2016.

The gallery is sprawled across an art deco building (*see page 74*). It focuses on contemporary Moroccan art, collaborating with artists – who are often invited to stay on-site – from initial concept to realisation. The exhibitions change every two months and run the gamut of paintings and sculptures to installations.
62 Rue Yougoslavie
+212 (0)6 6301 0191
comptoirdesminesgalerie.com

Matisse Art Gallery, Gueliz
Mixed exhibits

Matisse Art Gallery opened in 1999 in the Passage Ghandouri, a stone's throw from Macma (*see page 63*). Ever since, the two floors behind its black-marble façade have played host to some of the most renowned names on the Moroccan art scene – including Farid Belkahia, Mahi Binebine and Hassan El Glaoui – as well as up-and-coming artists.
Passage Ghandouri,
61 Rue Yougoslavie
+212 (0)5 2444 8326

❸
David Bloch Gallery, Gueliz
Spirited collaboration

The sleek façade of this ground-floor Gueliz gallery is lined with floor-to-ceiling windows that provide a good view of the contemporary art within. Inside, white walls are paired with a polished concrete floor. The building was abandoned before David Bloch, who first came to Marrakech on holiday in the 1990s, bought and refurbished it in time for the opening of his gallery in 2010.

"We're a promotion gallery," says Bloch, "meaning we foster long-term collaborations with artists." Some 20 international names are represented – both emerging and established – and they're given free rein when it comes to solo exhibitions.
8 Bis Rue des Vieux Marrakchis
+212 (0)5 2445 7595
davidblochgallery.com

Solo show
—
Tucked away in the heart of the medina, Riad Yima is the studio, gallery, shop and tea room of Hassan Hajjaj. Every surface is covered with the well-known artist's work, from photographs that capture Arab life to furniture made from recycled African signs.
riadyima.com

Left a bit, right a bit

⑤

Voice Gallery, Ménara
Breeding ground

For Italian Rocco Orlacchio (*pictured*), running a gallery is about creating a community of talent from disparate backgrounds. He works with local and international artists, most of whom are young and engaged with what's going on around the world, be it politically, environmentally or socially. Moroccan artist M'Barek Bouhchichi, for example, creates artwork from leftover plastic.

Orlacchio chose Marrakech because at the time, in 2011, its art scene was in flux – and that's the kind of shaky ground on which great art is often made. In 2019 the gallery moved into this giant former jam factory.
Rue Salah Eddine Al Ayoubi
+212 (0)6 5848 2800
voicegallery.net

Fair game

It wasn't until Vanessa Branson (sister to Richard) set up the Marrakech Biennale in 2004 that a spotlight, albeit a rather patchy one, began to shine on the Moroccan art scene. It sparked a dialogue between local and international art communities, and promoted cultural venues across the city.

When the seventh edition, due to be held in February 2018, was cancelled due to a lack of funds, it was a big disappointment. But the arrival of Moroccan native Touria El Glaoui's 1-54 Contemporary African Art Fair that same month lessened the blow. With a solid reputation in global art centres, 1-54 attracts collectors from all over.
marrakechbiennale.org;
1-54.com/marrakech

Foundations and
cultural centres
Ambitious aims

❶
Montresso Art Foundation,
Ouidane
Artist retreat

Getting to this vibrant art
foundation is a bit of a mission:
though only 20km from the
city, it's well and truly off the
beaten track, at the heart of
an olive grove. Established
by Jean-Louis Haguenauer in
1981, it promotes Moroccan
art and culture through the
Jardin Rouge artists residency
and the Montresso Art Space.

The Jardin Rouge
was established in 2009
and welcomes up to 30
international artists a year,
allowing them to develop and
experiment while receiving
support. The gallery space – a
magnificent modern structure –
was founded in 2016 and hosts
contemporary art exhibitions.
It's open by appointment on
Fridays and Saturdays; sign
up for a tour of the entire
complex, including the studios.
Douar Ouled Zbir, Route de Fès
+212 (0)5 2980 1592
montresso.com

②

Le 18, Medina
Contemporary meets traditional

Laila Hida (*pictured*) was born in Casablanca, studied in Paris and worked as a photographer and producer before setting up Le 18 in 2013. Her foundation started out as an experimental space for the odd exhibition as well as talks about art, society and politics. It now offers a consistent annual programme.

The setting is a renovated riad in the medina – a far cry from the white-cube galleries of Gueliz. It offers a different perspective on contemporary art. "We want to move forward with our history," says Hida. Le 18 puts on four exhibitions a year and also has a rolling residency programme.
18 Derb El Ferrane
+212 (0)5 2438 9864
le18marrakech.com

③

Dar Bellarj, Medina
Flight of fancy

A pocket of calm in the medina, Dar Bellarj has a schedule stuffed with wide-ranging events. Temporary exhibitions have taken on themes such as embroidery, scents and the art of stucco. Workshops might hone in on calligraphy or theatre, and past concerts have presented Sufi music.

The building too has been through many iterations – hospital, private residence, school – and is even said to have once been a sanctuary for injured storks (hence the name *bellarj*, which translates as "stork" in Arabic). In the early 2000s the complex was bought by Swiss architects Susanna Biedermann and Max Alioth, who set up the foundation.

There's no entrance fee and during Ramadan the institution hosts evening concerts in its central courtyard.
7-9 Toualat Zaouiat Lahdar
+212 (0)5 2444 4555

Cinemas
Take a picture

②

Cinéma le Colisée, Gueliz
Curtain call

This cinema has a lot to live up to: it was built in 1953 according to a design by Georges Peynet, the French architect behind Parisian cinemas such as Max Linder Panorama and Vendôme-Opéra. The entrance features a ribbed ceiling that resembles a swept-back curtain – a nod to the revelatory nature of the screening rooms within.

Refurbished in 1995, Cinéma le Colisée offers a varied programme of films often shown in their original language, including English, with French subtitles. It's also one of the hosts of the Festival International du Film de Marrakech (*see page 138*).
Boulevard Mohammed Zerktouni
+212 (0)5 2444 8893

①

Cinéma Leila Alaoui,
Camp El Ghoul
Different perspectives

A collaboration between the Fondation Leila Alaoui – established to preserve the humanitarian efforts of the late French-Moroccan video artist and photographer – and the Institut Français de Marrakech, the Cinéma Leila Alaoui was inaugurated in 2017. The former theatre of the institute has been transformed into a picture house that showcases French arthouse cinema, documentary films and international flicks.

In line with Alaoui's work – which explores themes such as the construction of identity and migration – the cinema aims to foster cultural diversity through imagery and film.
Route de la Targa Jbel Guéliz
+212 (0)5 2444 6930
if-maroc.org

Movie night
———
The Musée Yves Saint Laurent's (*see page 64*) Ciné-Club screens the fashion designer's favourite films at 19.00 every Thursday. Expect 20th-century classics by the likes of Jean Cocteau and Orson Welles.
museeyslmarrakech.com

①
Media
Fresh pages

Morocco may have its fair share of French and Arabic papers but many are state-owned and, as such, restricted when it comes to news coverage. Imprisonment and persecution of independent journalists who question the government is commonplace.

Our round-up of the best titles to peruse is focused on French-language publications produced across the country.

Founded by Hassan Alaoui in 2015, **①** *Maroc Diplomatique* is a monthly newspaper filled with reports, interviews and surveys on various social, political and cultural issues. **②** *L'Économiste*, the independent sister publication of Arabic daily *Assabah*, provides a regular dose of economic and financial news. **③** *L'Opinion* is another daily – but published in Rabat – focusing on general news, economics and politics. Casablanca-based **④** *Le Matin*, which first hit presses in 1971 and is perhaps the most accessible of the French-language papers, brings together sport, world news, economics, celebrity gossip, politics and general-interest topics. Another politically independent, general-interest daily is **⑤** *Aujourd'hui*.

Weekly magazine **⑥** *Tel Quel* is marked by its brave coverage of the politics of the day and its investigative reporting, plus its progressive take on international relations, economics and culture.

Founded in 1995, **⑦** *Femmes du Maroc* is a monthly magazine published in Casablanca and directed by Moroccan journalist Aïsha Zaïmi Sakhri, a big supporter of women's rights. It features fashion and beauty pages and also interviews with politicians and artists, as well as reports on the Moroccan social scene. **⑧** *VH magazine*, short for "Version Homme", was established as a monthly lifestyle and culture magazine for men in 2002.

⑨ *Diptyk* is the country's premier arts title, dedicated to documenting Arabic and African contemporary art. Six issues a year cover major events in both the Moroccan and international art world, with reviews and artist profiles. And finally we have **⑩** *Chergui*, an in-house journal published twice a year by cultural foundation Le 18 (*see page 69*). An extension of the physical space, it takes on a different theme each time and features writing from contributors around the world in various languages.

Design and architecture
—— Built environment

Architecturally speaking, Marrakech is relatively homogeneous – beautiful but predictable. Those looking for sparkling new structures are likely to be disappointed: contemporary projects are rare, and beyond the brickwork brilliance of the Musée Yves Saint Laurent there is little to excite. Even the "new" town of Gueliz is relatively dated by the standards of most cities, although its art deco streets are certainly worth a wander.

Without a doubt the city's drawcard is its swathe of pre-20th-century structures, from the towering minarets of its mosques to the ostentatious ornamentation of its palaces. Prepare for your jaw to well and truly drop.

Marrakech is also remarkably verdant – the Atlas Mountains, which sit just beyond the skyline like a mirage, have provided the city with its vital water supply for centuries, and its courtyards teem with plants and flowers that defy the dry terrain. In fact, the gardens define the city as much as its buildings so we've included our pick of the bunch here.

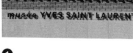

❶

Musée Yves Saint Laurent,
Majorelle
Fashion house

This 2017 building by Studio
KO is one of the city's only
examples of contemporary
architecture – and certainly
the finest. Housing a museum
(*see page 64*) dedicated to
Yves Saint Laurent, the
low-slung structure blends
chameleon-like with its
surroundings due to the
slabs of smooth rose granite
and earthy red brickwork,
which is designed to evoke
the texture of woven fabric.

Visitors walk down a cool
corridor to a temple-like
courtyard where oblongs of
coloured glass surround the
unmistakable YSL logo and the
sky is framed in a dramatic
circle above.
Rue Yves Saint Laurent
+212 (0)5 2429 8686
museeyslmarrakech.com

❷

Aéroport Marrakech Ménara
extension, Ménara
Flights of fancy

The brief for this extension
to the city's airport, which
was completed between 2006
and 2008, was to give visitors
a modern experience while
employing a design that drew
on traditional Moroccan motifs.
The structure is defined by a
series of giant interconnected
concrete rhombuses inlaid with
frosted glass panels decorated
with intricate arabesque patterns.

In another part of the
building a corrugated brise-soleil
perforated with eight-pointed
stars ripples across the façade.
As the fierce Moroccan sun
filters through, casting patterned
shadows onto the polished floor,
the effect is both traditional yet
resolutely modern.
Rak Mhamid
+212 (0)5 2444 7910
marrakesh-airport.com

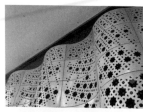

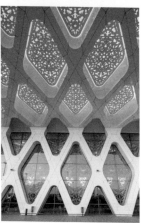

20th century
Modernist marvels

1

Comptoir des Mines Galerie,
Gueliz
Art deco insides

This peachy building from
1932 was originally owned
by the Comptoir des Mines
mining company but now
houses a gallery space
(*see page 65*) conceived by
Hicham Daoudi, founder of
the Marrakech Art Fair. The
exterior is elegant in its angular
simplicity but the real draw
is the sensitively restored art
deco interior: think white-
black-and-gold colour palette,
terrazzo flooring, fan-shaped
crystal wall lamps and
sweeping spiral staircases.
62 Rue Yougoslavie
+ 212 (0)6 6301 0191
comptoirdesminesgalerie.com

*Let's hope it's
not a mirage!*

❸
Résidence Anouar housing
project, Hivernage
Home visit

This building employs a
clever concertina-like indented
floor plan to maximise space
and create double orientations
for the apartments within.
Designed by Abdeslem Faraoui
and Patrice de Mazières, it
was constructed on a corner
plot in a residential area of
Hivernage between 1960 and
1970. The concrete exterior
has an earthy ochre finish
and the latticed window frames
– which in many cases have
sadly been neglected to the
point of disrepair – are made
of cedar wood.
*Avenue Echouhada and
Rue Ibn Khafajah*

❷

Petrol station, Gueliz
Hit the gas

On a traffic-choked intersection
in Gueliz sits an unlikely
monument to modernism: a
gleaming petrol station that
shines like a toothy grin among
the terracotta buildings that
surround it. The structure was
designed in 1958 by Jean-
François Zevaco, a French-
Moroccan architect from
Casablanca who is credited
with introducing modernist
architecture to his homeland.

The defining feature of the
petrol station is its soaring white
concrete roof, which shades
the forecourt with a sculptural
simplicity reminiscent of the
work of Mexican-Spanish
architect Félix Candela.
Although perhaps not thrilling
enough to warrant a journey
in itself, the site's proximity to
the Musée Yves Saint Laurent
(*see pages 64 and 72 to 73*) and
Jardin Majorelle (*see page 80*)
means it can easily be visited in
conjunction with other places.
*Corner of Avenue Yacoub El
Mansour and Rue Al Madina*

Pre-20th century
Grand affair

④
Église des Saints Martyrs,
Gueliz
Take me to church

Morocco became a French
protectorate in 1912 and army
general Hubert Lyautey was
tasked with managing the
urban development that would
house the subsequent influx of
Europeans. Keen to preserve
the historic medina, he turned
his attention to the area to the
northwest of the centre – what
is now Gueliz. The 1928 Église
des Saints Martyrs (Church of
the Holy Martyrs) was the first
church to be built in Marrakech
and fuses art deco and moorish
influences, all in the classic
shade of salmon pink.
Rue El Imam Ali
+212 (0)5 2443 0585

①
Palais Bahia, Medina
Picture-perfect palace

This labyrinthine complex
of courtyards, colonnades
and high-ceilinged reception
halls was built and expanded
throughout the 19th century,
mainly at the request of grand
vizier Bou Ahmed, who added
quarters for his four wives and
24 concubines. *Bahia* is roughly
translated as "beautiful" or
"brilliant" and the palace
certainly lives up to its name.
A true visual assault, expect
intricate tiling, lush gardens
and striped ceilings in bold
primary colours that look
almost contemporary.
Avenue Imam El Ghazali
+212 (0)5 2438 9179
palais-bahia.com

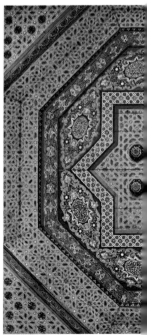

2

Mosquée Koutoubia, Medina
Tallest tower

The largest mosque – and one of the oldest buildings – in Marrakech, the mighty Mosquée Koutoubia has cast its impressive shadow across the western part of the medina since the late 12th century (the first mosque on the site was completed in 1157 but later demolished as it was not correctly aligned with Mecca).

The cavernous structure can accommodate some 25,000 worshippers at any one time. City laws prohibit the construction of anything taller than the minaret – which, if you believe the legends, only blind muezzins were permitted to climb because the balcony at the top offered prime views of the royal harem.

Rue Ibn Khaldoun
+212 (0)6 4472 7244
mosquee-koutoubia.com

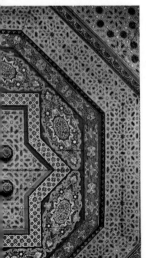

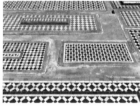

 3

Tombeaux Saadiens, Kasbah
Laid to rest

Here lie the remains of anyone
who was anyone during
the reign of the Saadians,
the dynasty that governed
Morocco from 1549 to 1659.
No expense was spared
in the construction of the
mausoleums: they are packed
to the intricately carved
rafters with Cararra marble,
kaleidoscopic tiles and gold.
 After the fall of the Saadians
the tombs were sealed off
and lay forgotten for more
than 200 years; in 1917
they were rediscovered
through aerial photography.
Rue de la Kasbah
+212 (0)5 2437 8163
tombeaux-saadiens.com

④

Ramparts
Writing's on the wall

While the origins of some monikers have become murky over time, there's no mistaking the source of the nickname "the Red City". One of the first things visitors to Marrakech will notice on approaching the city are the imposing ramparts which encircle the medina.

Made from coral-coloured clay known as pisé, the walls – the construction of which began in 1126 – stretch for some 19km and are punctuated with gates (which until the early 20th century were securely fastened every night). The holes dotted across them are used to secure the scaffolding needed for their regular upkeep.

⑤

Palais El Badi, Medina
Royal flush

Sultan Ahmed al-Mansour of the Saadian dynasty (*see opposite*) decided that the only appropriate way to celebrate Morocco's victory over the Portuguese in the 1578 Battle of the Three Kings was to construct this enormous palace. He dedicated 25 years to the project, bedecking it with the finest gold, turquoise, marble and crystal he could lay his hands on.

Its opulence was short-lived: less than 75 years later it was ransacked by Moulay Ismail and today the site is little more than an atmospheric shell. The entrance isn't entirely obvious either: head for Place des Ferblantiers and follow the ramparts along to the right.
Ksibat Nhass
+212 (0)5 2437 8163
palais-el-badi.com

Gardens
Great outdoors

❶
Jardin Majorelle, Majorelle
Out of the blue

This garden is far from a hidden gem: a visit will require you to circumnavigate crowds of camera-toting tourists (get here early to avoid the snaking queues). But it should make it onto your itinerary whether or not you're a budding botanist.

The electric-blue art deco villa at its centre was designed by architect Paul Sinoir in 1931 for the French painter Jacques Majorelle, who used it as his studio. The garden – which Majorelle filled with exotic species collected on his travels – fell into disrepair after his death in 1962. Eighteen years later it was bought by Yves Saint Laurent and Pierre Bergé, who restored it to its former vibrant glory.
Rue Yves Saint Laurent
+212 (0)5 2429 8686
jardinmajorelle.com

2

Le Jardin Secret, Medina
Two in one

This lavish riad was originally built for the kaid Al-Hajj Abd-Allah U-Bihi in the mid-19th century. He didn't get to enjoy it for long – suspected of political intrigue, he was poisoned and his home passed from ruler to ruler until, in the 1930s, the garden became increasingly unkempt and overgrown. In 2013, British landscape architect Tom Stuart-Smith was brought in to restore it.

There are two distinct areas: the Exotic Garden hosts plants sourced everywhere from Mexico to Madagascar, while the Islamic Garden presents Morocco's floral bounty including lavender, rosemary, fig, olive and orange trees.
121 Rue Mouassine
+212 (0)5 2439 0040
lejardinsecretmarrakech.com

3

Musée de la Palmeraie, Annakhil
Prickly encounter

In sharp (spiky, if you will) contrast to Jardin Majorelle (*see opposite*), this garden and gallery complex is so far off the beaten track that your taxi driver may struggle to find it. Founded by garden designer, ethnobotanist, perfumer and photographer Abderrazzak Benchaâbane in 2011, the Musée de la Palmeraie is a world away from the medina.

Skip the gallery part and head straight to the gardens, which are laid out in various sections. Our favourite, the cactus garden, is planted with some 40 different kinds of cacti from Morocco, South Africa and the Americas and is dotted with metal sculptures.
Route de Fès
+212 (0)6 6109 5352
benchaabane.com/musee_palmeraie

Sculpture vultures
—
Multimedia artist André Heller has created a botanical wonderland studded with sculptures 27km from Marrakech in the Ourika Valley. A shuttle bus (included in the ticket price) runs from the Koutoubia car park to Anima Garden a few times daily.
anima-garden.com

Visual identity
Snapshots of the city

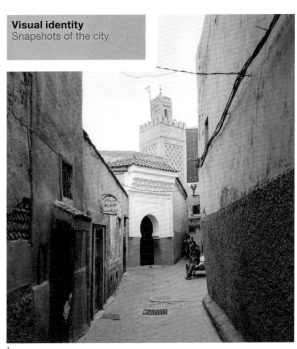

1

2

3

4

5

6

7

8

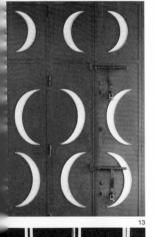

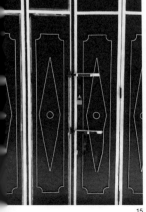

1 — 5 The Red City: The colour of the city's walls was once dictated by the pisé clay used to construct them (*see page 79*) but when the French arrived and started building with new materials, laws were passed to ensure that this consistency continued. Now you'll find every shade of "red", from rust and terracotta to salmon, coral and peach.

6 — 7 Lanterns: Few things say "Marrakech" quite so evocatively as a lantern casting a soft glow and sending patterned shadows dancing around a courtyard.

8 Two wheels: Keep your wits about you when exploring the medina – there's no escaping the incessant buzz of scooters, mopeds and motorbikes.

9 — 12 Tiles: Floors, walls, fountains, sinks and doorways: few surfaces in the city escape the tile treatment. Marrakech is an expert in *zellige*: a mosaic technique that sees geometric tiles set in plaster.

13 — 16 Metal doors: Unlike with the city's walls, there are no restrictions on what can be done with the ubiquitous metal doors. You'll find plenty of playful designs.

Sport and fitness
—— Let's get physical (ish)

Simply navigating the streets of the medina in the heat of the day is enough to build up a sweat, so you'll want to balance it out with a hefty dose of rest and relaxation, whether it be cooling off in one of Beldi Country Club's turquoise-tiled pools, unwinding in the hot tub of a luxurious hotel spa or taking some deep, meditative breaths at a rooftop yoga class. Don't bother packing your running shoes – this is not a city for joggers.

❶
Beldi Country Club, Chrifia
Beat a retreat

A dusty country road just outside the city leads to this idyllic country club. Surrounded by 15 hectares of lush gardens, Beldi boasts three outdoor swimming pools as well as a particularly decadent covered option for when the temperatures drop (complete with a chandelier overhead and blazing fireplace at one end).

Visitors can also book in for lessons at Beldi's tennis court or unwind with a traditional Moroccan scrub at the spacious hammam and spa. For those keen to stay a little longer in this peaceful spot, Beldi also has its own on-site hotel where you can bed down for the night.
Km 6, Route de Barrage
+212 (0)5 2438 3950
beldicountryclub.com

❷
Toubkal National Park
Ain't no mountain higher

For a real sense of escape, look no further than Toubkal National Park. This awe-inspiring range of rocky valleys, Berber villages and craggy peaks is just 70km outside Marrakech and home to the highest mountain in north Africa, the 4,000-metre-tall Jbel Toubkal. For less-experienced hikers, there are plenty of paths criss-crossing the mountainsides.

Multi-day trips to Toubkal are offered by groups such as Atlas and Sahara Tours, which also organises guides to lead the way and prepares picnics to keep walkers fuelled.
atlasandsaharatours.com

Inner-city oases
Hit refresh

❶
Heritage Spa, Medina
Take five

Weary souk shoppers can
enjoy a well-earned break in
this elegant retreat. As well as
massages and argan-oil facials,
the spa offers three different
hammam experiences – each of
which features a vigorous scrub
followed by a deep-cleansing
ghassoul mask made using a
mineral-rich clay found only
in Morocco.

Traditionally decorated and
dimly lit treatment rooms are
spread throughout the riad's
central courtyard, where guests
kick back with a sweet mint
tea between treatments.
40 Arset Aouzal
+212 (0)5 2438 4333
heritagespamarrakech.com

Hotel spas

01 **Amanjena, Annakhil:**
This decadent spa has
five treatment rooms
for massages and more,
all using Aman's own
skincare range. The hotel
also has two marble-clad
hammams where both
guests and non-guests
can unwind as part of
half and full-day retreats.
aman.com/amanjena.

02 **La Mamounia, Medina:**
In keeping with the
rest of the hotel (*see
page 17*), this spa is
steeped in old-school
glamour. It's centred
around a lavish indoor
pool and features
a lantern-lit treatment
area where visitors
can experience La
Mamounia's signature
argan-oil massage.
mamounia.com

03 **Royal Mansour,
Medina:** Intricate
Moorish latticework lines
the walls of this highly
picturesque spa at the
Royal Mansour (*see page
16*). With 10 treatment
rooms it's one of the
largest in the city and a
vast team of masseuses,
beauticians, hair stylists
and podiatrists are on
hand to make sure you
have everything you need.
royalmansour.com

Yippee!

②

The Flow, Medina
Strike a pose

Perfect your downward-facing dog at this tranquil studio in the medina. The bright-and-airy space at Riad Be offers three sessions of vinyasa yoga a day (morning, afternoon and evening), with spaces available on a drop-in basis.

Sessions also take place on the riad's sunny rooftop terrace, where yoga mats are rolled out over berber rugs and yogis can admire views across the city while they practise. Private sessions are available for those looking for one-to-one guidance.

23 Derb Sidi Lahcen o Ali
+212 (0)5 2438 4511
theflowyogastudio.com

Hot and steamy
—

Hammams date back to the Ottomans as public baths, often used before prayer. They remain an important part of Moroccan culture; not just for those looking to relax and cleanse but also as a place for communities to gather and gossip inside their steamy chambers.

Walk
—— Take to the streets

You could walk the medina of Marrakech every day and stumble across something new each time. We've devised an easy-to-follow trail that takes in all the major sites, plus a couple of lesser-known treasures, to give you a full dose of everything this brilliantly chaotic part of town has to offer.

And if you do stray from the path, don't worry – the medina's charms in part lie in chance discoveries. So allow yourself to get a little lost, we won't be offended.

Medina
Old-town tour

Kick things off outside the 12th-century **1** *Mosquée Koutoubia* (*see page 77*) straight after breakfast. If the *Adhan* (call to prayer) has been keeping you up at night, it's probably the one coming from this mighty minaret. Non-Muslims can't go in to appreciate the architecture but there's plenty to enjoy from the outside.

Continue onto **2** *Jemaa El Fna*, which should have just enough bustle at this time of day without having descended into chaos: a fine moment to grab a mint tea on the patio of one of the cafés, and watch the street chefs set up their stalls.

Head to the north side of the square and find Souk Laksour, one of the main arteries that girdle the medina. It's lined

with all manner of shops, selling everything from brass lamps to amateur watercolours depicting the city.

Take a right once you reach a café called Le Bougainvillier, then turn left and you'll soon come to **3** *Le Jardin Secret* (*see page 81*). Both the garden and the palace in which it resides have gradually evolved since the 16th century but what you see now is a faithful restoration of their 19th-century incarnation. Plants from five continents grow root-to-root here and are fed by the original underground channels that bring water from the Atlas Mountains. Take some time to enjoy the serenity.

Retrace your steps and take a left when you hit the T-junction. Next to a restaurant called Terrasse de la Fontaine is an arched entrance into the **4** *Souk des Tailleurs de Pierre*. It's much calmer than the other souks and has a broad selection

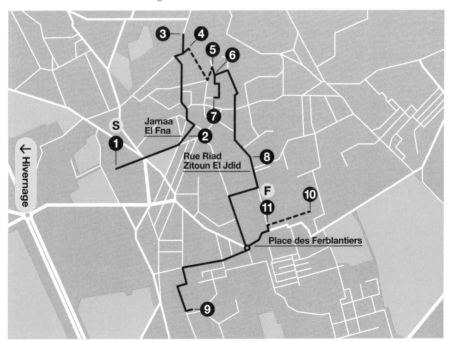

– the glassware is particularly good. Wander around then follow the overhead signs to Nomad (*see page 30*), which will bring you to Rahba Lakdima. You have two options for a quick drink: there's the tucked-away **5** *ChiChaoua Tea Room* (*see page 39*) or Café des Épices (*see page 38*) next door. Once sated, cross the square and pop into **6** *Chabi Chic*, which sits on the ground floor of Nomad. It stocks pretty homeware that adds a modern (and at times kitsch) twist to the Moroccan style.

Speaking of kitsch, exit right and a couple of twists and turns will bring you to **7** *Riad Yima* (*see page 66*). The gallery-shop sells the artwork and designs of Morocco's most renowned artist, Hassan Hajjaj. It's pretty loud stuff but it makes for an entertaining tour, whether you're purchasing something or not.

Retrace your steps back to Place Rahba Lakdima, walk to the eastern side and then stroll south down Znikat Rahba (the road on which the Musée du Patrimoine is located, if you need a landmark). The streets get narrower and yet more atmospheric here. Within minutes you'll reach Lebanese restaurant **8** *Naranj* (*see page 35*), where we recommend a lunch stop. Do save room for the halva mousse.

Exit left and look out for a long road on your right, which leads to the parallel-running Rue Riad Zitoun El Kdim; follow it until you leave the medina. A few shimmies west will then bring you to the Kasbah neighbourhood and the eerie **9** *Tombeaux Saadiens* (*see page 78*): a mid-16th century burial complex that was uncovered in 1917.

Not far from here, near Place des Ferblantiers, is the **10** *Palais Bahia* (*see page 76*), a brilliant 19th-century palace and former residence of the French chiefs in Morocco. If you've had enough culture and architecture for one day, next door is the somewhat surreal **11** *Restaurant El Bahia*, which has a little-known rooftop terrace and (a rarity in the medina) serves alcohol. Grab a Casablanca beer and enjoy the sunset.

Address book

01 Mosquée Koutoubia
Rue Ibn Khaldoun
+212 (0)6 4472 7244
mosquee-koutoubia.com

02 Jemaa El Fna

03 Le Jardin Secret
121 Rue Mouassine
+212 (0)5 2439 0040
lejardinsecretmarrakech.com

04 Souk des Tailleurs de Pierre
Rue Sidi El Yamani

05 ChiChaoua Tea Room
Rahba Lakdima
+212 (0)5 2433 8470

06 Chabi Chic
1 Derb Aarjane
+212 (0)5 2438 1546
chabi-chic.com

07 Riad Yima
52 Derb Aarjane
+212 (0)5 2439 1987
riadyima.com

08 Naranj
84 Rue Riad Zitoun El Jdid
+212 (0)5 2438 6805
naranj.ma

09 Tombeaux Saadiens
Rue de la Kasbah
+212 (0)5 2437 8163
tombeaux-saadiens.com

10 Palais Bahia
Rue Riad Zitoun El Jdid
+212 (0)6 7474 7464
palais-bahia.com

11 Restaurant El Bahia
1 Rue Riad Zitoun El Jdid
+212 (0)5 2437 8679
restaurantelbahia.com

Tangier

Elegant riads, rooftop bars, independent shops and art-house cinemas. Tangier, we salute you!

Welcome
—— Take a trip
to Tangier

Sexy but seedy, salacious yet civilised, sun-soaked Tangier has long attracted waves of colonisers. The city passed through the hands of the Portuguese, Spanish and British (and before that, the Phoenicians, Romans and Vandals) prior to becoming an "international zone" governed by mostly European powers for the first half of the 20th century, and its *chequered past* can be read in everything from its architecture to its cuisine. *Europe's gateway to Africa* – Spain is so close that it's visible across the Strait of Gibraltar – Tangier bridges the two continents seamlessly: mosques cosy up to catholic cathedrals and cafés spill out onto the pavement next to traditional Moroccan markets.

Socialites and artistic types have long been drawn to Tangier for its *freewheeling reputation, pleasant climes* and *colourful cultural scene*: creatives such as Henri Matisse, Tennessee Williams and Allen Ginsberg all found inspiration in its streets (and parties). The end of the 20th century saw the city's star fade somewhat as it became more synonymous with sleaziness than seduction, but over the past decade or so it has cleaned up its act.

Visitors today will find a *modern beach town* with bucketloads of charm. A slew of tasteful hotels, bookshops and boutiques have cropped up. While the medina remains a dusty tangle of winding streets, hop over the ramparts of the kasbah and you'll find a *bustling business district*, a *glittering new marina* and a long stretch of sand packed with paddling locals. So loosen a button or two and go with the flow – Tangier is used to playing the perfect host. — (M)

Map
—— The city at a glance

Tumbling down a steep cliff at the northwest tip of Africa, Tangier's topography is almost as dramatic as its history (*see opposite*). It's less than 35km across the Strait of Gibraltar from Tarifa in Spain, at the point where the mighty Atlantic meets the Mediterranean.

It's a compact city and, despite the inclines, easily navigable on foot – everything we list here is a quick walk from the centre of town. There are just three main neighbourhoods to acquaint yourself with. Much of the action is centred around

the medina – a tangle of narrow streets encircled by ancient ramparts. Unlike in Marrakech, this old town is scooter-free, making exploration here much more enjoyable. To the west is Marshan, where the avenues are wider and the houses bigger (and beyond that lies the Réserve du Cap Spartel and a string of unspoiled beaches).The city has its own popular crescent of sand, which backs onto the Ville Nouvelle – home to some of Tangier's best restaurants, retail spots and streetside cafés.

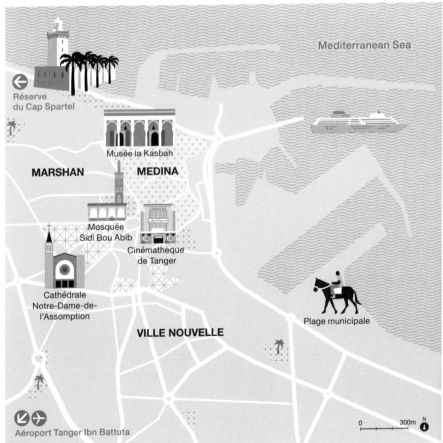

Mediterranean Sea

Réserve du Cap Spartel

Musée la Kasbah

MARSHAN

MEDINA

Mosquée Sidi Bou Abib

Cinémathèque de Tanger

Cathédrale Notre-Dame-de-l'Assomption

VILLE NOUVELLE

Plage municipale

Aéroport Tanger Ibn Battuta

0   300m   N

Need to know
—— Tangier talk

Popular culture
Hard to beat

Tangier has been a magnet for outlaws, eccentrics, misfits and dreamers for centuries, seduced by the city's laissez-faire attitude and cheap, exotic living. No wonder then that some of the 20th century's most eminent writers and creatives wound up here at some point or another.

The Beats were particularly partial to Tangier: Jack Kerouac, William S Burroughs and Allen Ginsberg all rolled through. Talking of rolling, Stones fans should make a pilgrimage to the rustic Café Baba (*see pages 98 to 99*).

History
Ups and downs

It might be easier to list the nations and civilisations that have *not*, at some point, laid claim on Tangier. A strategic position at the gateway to both the Med and the African continent has ensured the city's continued prosperity – but also its appeal in the eyes of aspiring conquerors.

After spells under Phoenician, Roman, Byzantine, Portuguese, Spanish and British rule, Tangier was declared an international zone in 1923 before finally falling back into the hands of the Moroccans after independence in 1956.

Want a ride?

Future development
New and improved

Change is once again afoot in this seaside city. A high-speed train link has shaved down journey time to Casablanca from almost five hours to just over two, a flashy new marina (Morocco's largest) and state-of-the-art fishing port were inaugurated in 2018 and the beachfront has been spruced up considerably. We get the feeling Tangier won't fly under the radar for much longer.

Noise
Sound it out

There are no two ways about it: Tangier is a noisy city. It may be the pre-dawn call to prayer, a belligerent feline staking its ground, an impassioned salesman advertising his wares in the souk or all three at once – but it's this clamour and commotion that make up the city's soundtrack. Our only advice? If you're staying in the medina and value your shut-eye, pack a pair of earplugs.

Hotels
Stay a while

1 2

3

4 5

6   7

8

9   10

1 — 2 Aux 3 Portes, Medina: Everywhere you turn in this six-room guesthouse is a riot of colours and patterns, with walls packed with intricately embroidered tapestries, ornately carved mirrors and mounted ceramics. Lush gardens extend beneath the hotel, leading down to a retro kidney-shaped pool. *aux3portes.com*

3 — 5 Dar Nour, Medina: A maze of staircases winds its way through this characterful B&B. The 10 bedrooms are decked out with traditional furnishings and eclectic artwork, while the roof terrace is lined with squashy white banquettes – perfect for an afternoon zizz. *darnour.com*

6 — 10 Hôtel Nord Pinus Tanger, Medina: Housed in an ancient riad at the highest point of the medina, this hotel boasts stellar views across the Strait of Gibraltar. Rooms feature ornate wrought-iron beds, stained-glass windows and elegant tiled bathrooms to boot. *nordpinustanger.com*

1

2

3

1 — 3 La Tangerina, Medina: This 10-room hotel is decorated with a mix of vintage finds from local flea markets and traditional fabrics from the nearby Rif region. The building itself is an elegantly renovated riad with a light-flooded central courtyard and picturesque roof terrace.
latangerina.com

4 — 5 Mimi Calpe, Ville Nouvelle: Built in the 1860s as the holiday home of a wealthy Moroccan family, Mimi Calpe looks like something straight out of the French Riviera. It's been faithfully preserved inside but new additions include a hammam and palm-tree-lined swimming pool.
mimicalpe.com

4   5

Food and drink
Wine and dine

1 **Gran Café de Paris, Ville Nouvelle:** Opened in 1927, this venerable café was once a hotspot for Tangier's literati and has welcomed the likes of Tennessee Williams and Jean Genet.
+212 (0)6 7421 1766

2 — 3 **Restaurant Hamadi, Medina:** Traditional Moroccan dishes are served in this sumptuously decorated restaurant to the sound of live Andalusian music played by its in-house band.
+212 (0)5 3993 4514

4 **Number One, Ville Nouvelle:** This low-key bar is housed in a renovated apartment and has an array of kitsch memorabilia displayed around its walls.
+212 (0)5 3994 1674

1 Saveur de Poisson, Ville Nouvelle: This small fish restaurant is a Tangier institution and well worth the inevitable queue. Don't expect a menu though – its offering depends on whatever comes off the boat that day.
+212 (0)5 3933 6326

2 — 4 Café Hafa, Marshan: Opened in 1921, this café tumbles down multiple tiers of whitewashed terraces overlooking the ocean. Tables are filled with locals sipping sweet mint tea and playing *parchís* (a popular board game in these parts).
Rue Hafa

5 — 8 Le Salon Bleu, Medina: A spiral staircase leads to the roof terrace of this small restaurant in the heart of the kasbah from the team behind Dar Nour (*see page 95*). Diners dig into plates of fried sardines with couscous against a blue-and-white backdrop.
+212 (0)6 6211 2724

9 Café Baba, Medina: Known as the spot where the Rolling Stones got stoned. Pictures of the famous clientele adorn the walls of this legendary cafe, which resembles something of a shabby time capsule from Tangier's rock'n'roll past. It's rough and ready but worth poking your nose in.
Rue Zaitouni

10 — 11 El Morocco Club, Medina: This renovated mansion encompasses three different venues: a sunny café terrace under the boughs of an ancient ficus tree, a dark wood-panelled piano bar and a sleek restaurant serving a fusion of Mediterranean and Moroccan cuisine.
elmoroccoclub.ma

1

2

3

4

5

6

9

7

8

10   11

Retail
Talking shop

1

2 3

4

5 6

7

8

9

10

11

1 — 3 Las Chicas, Marshan:
The closest thing you'll find to a concept store in Tangier, this well-appointed spot offers fashion, jewellery, homeware and cosmetics, plus a café area upstairs with a terrace.
+212 (0)5 3937 4510

4 — 6 Laure Welfling, Medina: This kitsch affair around the corner from the Musée la Kasbah (*see page 103*) is a real Aladdin's cave. Laure Welfling founded her eponymous fashion brand in Paris in 1978 and opened this boutique in 2001. You'll find her original designs alongside plenty of other treasures.
laurewelfling.com

7 — 8 Les Insolites, Ville Nouvelle: Born in Cannes, Stéphanie Gaou settled in Tangier in 2003 and opened this bookshop six years later in a former furniture restoration workshop. The space has since become an anchor of the city's cultural community, regularly hosting book signings, photography exhibitions, lectures and gigs.
+212 (0)5 3937 1367

9 Bleu de Fes, Medina:
In the market for a Berber carpet? Head to this shop set in a traditional house in the heart of the medina. Don't worry, it offers international shipping so you needn't have to lug your rug home.
bleudefes.com

10 — 11 Librairie des Colonnes, Ville Nouvelle: This bookshop first opened in 1949 and was later bought by Pierre Bergé. It has changed hands again since but still stocks a solid selection of titles in English, French and Arabic.
+212 (0)5 3993 6955

Culture
Sights and sounds

6

7

8

9

10 11

1 — 5 Cinémathèque de Tanger, Ville Nouvelle: New life was breathed into the art deco Cinéma Rif in 2007 when the renovated complex was reopened as a 425-seat cinema screening independent films from around the world as well as a range of old Moroccan flicks. The bar is an ever-popular hangout spot for the city's cool kids.
cinemathequedetanger.com

6 — 9 Musée la Kasbah, Medina: Housed in the former sultan's palace of Dar El Makhzen, this museum charts the history of the kasbah. Centred around a pretty tiled courtyard, its collection includes intricate Roman mosaics and an ornately gilded Quran from the 18th century.
fnm.ma/musee-de-la-kasbah-de-tanger

10 — 11 American Legation, Medina: This elegant five-storey mansion is the longest-serving US diplomatic building and today houses paintings and artefacts from the 19th and 20th centuries.
legation.org

Best of the rest
Treats around town

1 Cathédrale Notre-Dame-de-l'Assomption, Ville Nouvelle: The Tangier skyline is punctuated by the towers and minarets of numerous places of worship – a sign of the city's multifaceted history and inter-religious tolerance. The geometric steeple of this Roman Catholic church is the most striking of the bunch.
Avenue Ibn Al Haytem

2 Tombeaux Phéniciens, Marshan: Tangier was first settled by the Phoenicians as far back as the 8th century BC. These tombs carved out of the rock near Café Hafa (*see page 98*) are a popular sundown spot for locals snacking on popcorn and peanuts.

3 Mosquée Sidi Bou Abib, Ville Nouvelle: Built in 1917, this mosque on the edge of the palm-tree-fringed Grand Socco plaza is unusual for its salmon-pink minaret. Admire the kaleidoscopic tilework.
Place du 9 Avril

4 — 5 Plage Municipale, Ville Nouvelle: Tangier's strip of sand is pretty clean for a city beach and enduringly popular with residents, who come to socialise, play football and paddle.

6 — 8 Réserve du Cap Spartel and Atlantic beaches: Some 14km west of the city centre, a wooden sign marks the spot where the Atlantic meets the Med. This stretch of coastline boasts attractive beaches, a lush nature reserve and the cave where Hercules supposedly once took a nap.

1

2   3

4

5 6

7 8

Casablanca

Ahh, Casablanca. This seaside city is a classy affair. Join us for dinner, won't you?

Welcome
—— Casablanca calling

Ca-sa-blan-ca. Say it out loud. The very word conjures up an alluring image. To the fans of the 1942 Hollywood film, that vision is one of *dinner jackets* and *casinos*. And yes, you'll find a few of these here but the real Casablanca is something entirely more authentic, modern and enticing.

Visitors tend to shun Morocco's largest city in favour of Fez and Marrakech, or at best pop in as an afterthought – and how wrong they are. Casablanca is one of the gems of the Arabic-speaking world, a gleaming metropolis of *commerce, architecture* and *nightlife*. After undergoing rapid expansion during the French protectorate of 1912 to 1956, and later under a newly independent Morocco, it reinvented itself as a *global business hub* and the city of choice among north Africa's and the Middle East's most discerning.

It's a varied cityscape. Down by *La Corniche* are bars and clubs that throng until sunrise, just as kids kick off a game of football on the beach. Behind the port is the charming *Ancienne Medina* (old old town) that harks to the Morocco of yore. A short stroll away is the art deco-laden *Boulevard Mohammed V*, where architecture aficionados will crane their necks. Meanwhile, downtown commercial galleries showcasing African art rub shoulders with Japanese, French and Moroccan restaurants.

Casablanca is certainly a city that takes some time and effort to fully uncover and a little guidance doesn't go amiss. So allow us to present our rundown of the best that "Casa", as it's affectionately known, has to offer. *Bienvenus, nos amis.* — (M)

Map
—— Find a way

As with most cities, Casablanca's personality varies from neighbourhood to neighbourhood. To the west, in Ain Diab, you'll find the beach frequented by children playing football and families picnicking, as well as intrepid surfers riding the waves. Meanwhile, further east along the coast in El Hank you'll find the city's liveliest restaurants, bars and clubs.

Behind the port is the Ancienne Medina (old old town), which has a distinctly Mediterranean feel: think whitewashed buildings and winding alleys. A short walk east is Derb Omar and the Boulevard Mohammed V, a street lined with extraordinary art deco buildings. From here, hop in a taxi and head to the Habbous (the new medina), with its markets, shady squares and pleasant cafés.

Last but not least – and definitely worth a drive through – to the south of the city is Californie, which mimics the US state in both name and appearance, down to the lanky Washingtonia palms. A reminder of the strong war-time influence of the US in this city.

Atlantic Ocean

Mosquée Hassan II

EL HANK

SOUR JDID

ANCIENNE MEDINA

Plage Lalla Meryem

BOURGOGNE

AIN DIAB

ANFA

Boulevard Mohammed V

Grand Théâtre de Casablanca

DERB OMAR

La Villa Ronde

RACINE

Parc de la Ligue Arabe

LIBERTÉ

GAUTHIER

LA GIRONDE

LES HÔPITAUX

MAÂRIF

HABBOUS

0   500m   N

Aéroport Casablanca Mohammed V

Need to know
—— Background check

History
The sands of time

Nightlife
Bottoms up

Business hub
Money talks

Casablanca is Morocco's foremost business hub, and one of the most important in the Middle East and Africa too. According to the 2019 Global Financial Centres Index, it's the 22nd most desirable nucleus for business in the world – above the likes of Paris and Geneva – and the second in the AME region, behind only Dubai. As such, you can expect a wholly different crowd and atmosphere from that in Marrakech and Tangier.

Casablanca was originally known by the Berber name of Anfa, before being renamed Casa Branca some 60 years after the Portuguese sacked the city in 1515 (the current name is a Spanish variation). The city served as an important port during French colonial rule from 1912 to 1956, and it was the French who constructed the Habbous based on studies of extant traditional medinas. After Morocco's independence, Casa became the country's pre-eminent city, with Rabat serving only for administrative purposes. Mosquée Hassan II (*see page 117*) stands as a testament to the enormous importance that the monarchy places on the city.

Ok, starting to feel dizzy now

It's said that Casablancans head to Marrakech for the weekend to party but there's more Marrakshi hauteur in this than truth – after all, Casablanca has its own vibrant scene. Besides, alcohol restrictions are more relaxed thanks to the international crowd. It's normal here to see a Moroccan enjoying a drink or a boogie, as opposed to in more conservative Marrakech.

Getting around
Watch your step

Although the Habbous and Ancienne Medina make for wonderful promenades, as a whole Casablanca isn't fit for walking. Not only is it far too big but during its rapid expansion after independence the municipalities bisected the city with enormous roads and didn't take pedestrians into account. We recommend hailing a taxi to get around (*see page 139*).

Hotels
Hang your hat

1 3

4 5

6

7

1 — 3 Hôtel et Spa Le Doge, Place des Nations Unis: Built by an Italian entrepreneur in the 1930s, supposedly as a generous gift for his wife, this former townhouse was transformed into a hotel in 2010. Choose between 16 bedrooms, each of which is named after a 1930s figure and has wildly different decor. *hotelledoge.com*

4 — 5 Four Seasons Hotel Casablanca, Ain Diab: Casa's premier luxury hotel stands like a palace beside the ocean. It's the sort of hotel where your request is fulfilled before you've put down the phone. *fourseasons.com/casablanca*

6 — 9 Hôtel Central, Ancienne Medina: This whitewashed hotel was built in 1912 and sits on a quaint square in the Ancienne Medina. It had a new lick of paint in 2018 but retains its heritage, with original wrought-iron banisters and stained-glass windows. Plus, for the price, those airy balcony rooms are a steal. *hotelcentralcasa.com*

8   9

Food and drink
Table talk

1

2

3

5

6 7

8

10

11

9

12 13

1 — 5 Al Mounia, Liberté:
Escape Casablanca's heat in Al Mounia's leafy courtyard. The space as a whole is fit for a sultan (Jimmy Carter once ate here – close enough). The cuisine is traditional: think vegetable-focused tagines and meaty *tangias*.
+212 (0)5 2222 2669

6 — 8 Iloli, Gauthier:
A Japanese restaurant in Casablanca good enough to give Tokyo a run for its money? This is not a mirage. Best of all, Noëlle Bouayad and Yusuke Furukawa's Iloli combines the casual, hearty dishes of an izakaya – such as *donburi* (a rice bowl with meat, fish or vegetables) – with the elevated sensibilities of a sushi restaurant.
iloli-restaurant.com

9 — 14 Umayya, El Hank:
This Middle Eastern-style joint perches on a cluster of rocks above the ocean, providing a stunning view while you tuck into your dinner. The portions are more than generous and the speciality is fresh fish. Stick around until after midnight when the venue turns into one of Casa's most happening bars.
umayya.ma

14

1

2

3

4

5

6

7

8

9

1 — 6 Le Cabestan, El Hank:
This sumptuous space
– a bit exotic, a bit 1970s –
overlooks the ocean and is a
spirited affair come sundown,
whether you're here for a
long and leisurely dinner or
a quick nightcap. Crucially,
Le Cabestan also serves one
of the best Negronis in town.
le-cabestan.com

**7 Bondi Coffee Kitchen,
Gauthier:** Yearning for
a good cup of coffee in a
country where mint tea rules
supreme? Aussie Justina
Tulloch's café serves the
silkiest flat whites and has
a linger-all-day atmosphere.
+212 (0)6 5168 7707

**8 — 13 Pâtisserie Bennis,
Habbous:** To throw a party
in Casablanca and not order
pastries from Pâtisserie
Bennis is nothing short of
sacrilege. Grab a selection
and don't miss the *corne
de gazelle* (an almond-and-
orange-blossom-filled delight
shaped like a gazelle horn).
patisseriebennis.business.site

11

10

12 13

Culture
Get the picture

1 — 2 **Villa des Arts, Gauthier:** Modern art in an elegant whitewashed villa that dates back to the 1930s. This public gallery is run by the not-for-profit ONA Foundation, which promotes cultural diversity.
fondationona.ma

3 **L'Atelier 21, Racine:** A commercial gallery that champions both established and emerging artists from the continent and its diaspora.
atelier21.ma

4 — 5 **Loft Art Gallery, Racine:** Founded by sisters Yasmine and Myriem Berrada Sounni in 2009, this is one of Casablanca's best-known galleries and a key platform for Moroccan modern art.
loftartgallery.net

1   2

3   4   5

Design and architecture
Striking structures

1

2

4

3

5

1 — 4 Mosquée Hassan II, Sour Jdid: Completed in 1993 to commemorate King Hassan II's 60th birthday, this mind-boggling mosque is crowned with a 60-storey minaret and comprises highly intricate woodwork and heated marble floors. Sign up for one of several daily tours.
mosquee-hassan2.com

5 La Villa Ronde, Anfa: This villa was completed in 1965 by German architect Wolfgang Ewerth and, according to myth, slowly rotates (it doesn't). Though privately owned, it occasionally opens to the public.
Rue d'Anfa Supérieur

1

2

3

4

5

6

7   8

1 Église du Sacré Coeur, Place des Nations Unis: Built by the French in 1930, this church became a cultural centre after Morocco's independence. Look out for temporary exhibitions and performances.
Corner of Rue d'Alger and Boulevard Rachdi

2 — 3 Boulevard Mohammed V, Derb Omar: A veritable open-air museum of art deco architecture, erected during the French protectorate between 1912 and 1956.
Boulevard Mohammed V

4 Cinéma Rialto, Derb Omar: This old-school single-screen cinema is housed in an art deco building (with stellar signage) that dates back to the 1930s.
20 Rue Mohammed El Quorri

5 Grand Théâtre de Casablanca, Place des Nations Unis: The flagship architectural project of 21st-century Morocco cost more than €134m to build and opened in September 2019.
Avenue Hassan II

6 Église Notre-Dame de Lourdes, Les Hôpitaux: One of only two Catholic churches in Casablanca, this one was completed in 1956. Inside is an impressive and elaborate stained-glass series by French artist Gabriel Loire.
dioceserabat.org/paroisses

7 — 8 AXA Assurance building, Gauthier: This hedgehog-like office block, completed in 1979, is one of the masterpieces by French-Moroccan modernist architect Jean-François Zevaco.
120-122 Avenue Hassan II

Best of the rest
Walk this way

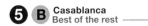

6

1 — 5 Ancienne Medina: Casablanca's medina is divided into old (Ancienne Medina) and new (Habbous). While the latter – built by the French in the 1930s – may be a little cleaner and more laid-back, don't leave without a stroll through the labyrinthine alleyways of the oldest area in the city. Sandwiched between the port and the Mosquée Hassan II.

6 — 10 La Corniche, Ain Dab: When you grow tired of the tower blocks and traffic-choked streets, make a beeline for this oceanfront boulevard – a cooling stretch that wraps around the windswept coast. Though its sandy beaches are a tad grittier than those in Tangier, they're popular with residents and visitors alike. Mosey as far as the El Hank lighthouse then take a dip in the ocean – just bear in mind that the waves are often big and, as a result, brimming with surfers.

7

8 9

10

6 essays
—— Musings
on Morocco

ESSAY 01
Change of scenery
Moroccan geography
——

Come take a journey
around Morocco's many
and varied landscapes,
from sun-scorched
deserts and craggy
coastlines to snowy
mountain ranges that
reach for the skies.

by James Clark,
writer

The written history of Morocco dates back to the eighth century BC, when the Phoenicians arrived from what's now called Lebanon. But native Amazigh people, commonly known as Berbers, were here about 2,000 years before that.

In more modern times, Sultan Mohammed V successfully negotiated Moroccan Independence in 1956, establishing a monarchy in 1957 and an elected government in 1958. Further unrest followed but the Morocco of today was gradually recognised.

Despite centuries of disorder, many Moroccan landscapes look the same as they did when the Phoenicians first settled. It's an unspoiled, varied land. The year-round sunshine, lively seaside towns, Sahara Desert, imperial cities and Atlas Mountains attract wide-eyed visitors from around the world.

The Rif is a dramatic mountainous region filled with fertile gorges that extends from Tangier in the west to the Moulouya River in the east and the Mediterranean

Sea in the north to the Ouargha River in the south. It offers mountain-edge views of the Mediterranean Sea for many of its 290km. You may expect a dry and arid land but the Rif is surprisingly lush in parts, with pine forests, seasonal flowers and other vegetation. The highest peak is the 2,456-metre-tall Mount Tidirhine, a popular hike.

The Atlas Mountains (divided into High and Anti) stretch across 2,500km and three countries – Morocco, Algeria and Tunisia – and separate the coastline from the Sahara Desert. They act as a weather barrier between the different ecosystems: if you were to visit all three countries in a day (yes, it's possible) you'd notice the climate change in each. The sheer size of this range provokes an emotional reaction. Though the High Atlas is just 95km from Marrakech, it feels a world away.

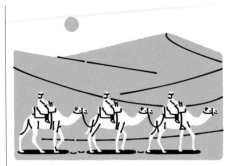

The canyons and ravines offer plentiful opportunities for hiking and mountain biking. Both come with their challenges but the sense of achievement as you hunker down for a good night's sleep in a traditional sunscorched Berber village at the end of a tough day is priceless. And don't be surprised if you're invited into a stone house for some sweetened mint tea along your route too – Berbers are friendly and hospitable people.

"Despite centuries of disorder, many Moroccan landscapes look the same as they did when the Phoenicians first settled"

At 4,167 metres high, Mount Toubkal is the highest peak in north Africa and capped with snow most of the year. Hikers make the three-day trek to the summit with guides, or you can opt to discover the region on mule or horseback. Set off from one of the wildflower valleys and drop by laid-back villages such as Oukaimeden. You'll find women perched on doorsteps baking homemade bread and men on the roadside selling honeycomb and *amlou*, a rich stone-milled spread of roasted almonds, argan oil and wild honey.

In the northwest Atlas the combination of fertile coastline, dry plateau and water at the base of the mountains creates the perfect environment for fig and pomegranate orchards. The landscape changes again when you reach the Sahara, famous for its vast sand dunes that rise up some 180 metres in height.

The desert offers a unique experience. It's possible to conquer the dunes on camels with the Walking with Nomads team, who will teach you everything you need to know about surviving in the desert, as nomadic tribes have for centuries. Sadly, due to climate change and marginalisation, this way of life has been all but lost.

Between the desert and the sea, you'll encounter several oases. Lush palm groves play an integral part in the climate, community and local economy. After the Sahara's heat, a stroll along the breezy Atlantic Mediterranean coast is just what you need. Coastal towns such as Agadir offer long sandy beaches, while the walled city of Essaouira has kitesurfing and shopping in its bustling medina. — (M)

ABOUT THE WRITER: James Clark is a UK-based travel journalist and writer focusing on adventure and the great outdoors. He loves nothing more than discovering new places and cultures.

ESSAY 02

Art for all
Contemporary art in Africa

────

The explosion of interest in contemporary African art in recent times has led to the rise of institutions keen to both promote and democratise access to it.

by Othman Lazraq, director of Fondation Alliances

The "rediscovery" of contemporary African art was first made outside Africa by the West. During the 1960s, art and culture were not our main priorities but fortunately things have changed. After our initial delay, we are catching up at a remarkable speed – though, if it were up to me, we would move even faster. We need to make it clear that there is no one artistic expression across the continent – there are many.

Contemporary African art has seen a monumental rise in popularity since the mid-2000s, resulting in skyrocketing prices and museums acquiring considerably more works by African artists. In turn, this has led to the birth of several institutions,

organisations and events that specialise in it, including Zeitz MOCAA in South Africa and 1-54 Contemporary African Art Fair in London, New York and now Marrakech. It's important that African art is being respected and discussed internationally – and it's just as important that this same discourse is now occurring in Africa itself. Today the continent is home to a host of art hubs such as Accra, Cape Town and, of course, Marrakech.

Located at the gateway between Europe and Africa, Morocco represents a major demographic and commercial crossroads. As for Marrakech, the city has become one of the most popular destinations on the continent, attracting an international, curious crowd.

I was born and raised in Casablanca but my heart has always been, and always will be, in Marrakech. My whole family has a very special relationship with this exceptional city – after all, it's where my parents' art collection was born. That's one of the reasons we founded our museum here.

My father and I opened the Musée d'Art Contemporain Africain Al Maaden (Macaal) in 2016 as one of the first private museums dedicated to contemporary African art. Starting in the 1980s, my parents built a collection of more than 2,000 works in about 40 years. In fact, they were among the first individuals in Morocco to collect Moroccan and African art. From our perspective, art is for everyone, which is why we decided to share it with the widest audience possible.

From a historic point of view, Marrakech has been a culturally and commercially bustling city since its foundation in 1071. But from the end of the 20th century, and exponentially from 2010, the offering of the city has been greatly enriched, notably thanks to the opening of world-class cultural and artistic institutions. Today the city has almost 20 museums and art foundations, and several more galleries; it hosts the Marrakech International Film Festival, theatre encounters, a contemporary dance festival, many music festivals, and, of course, the 1-54 Contemporary African Art Fair. Not to mention the countless cultural treasures tucked away around the city.

"My dream is to join forces with all the advocates of contemporary African art in order to create a platform that defends, supports and promotes art from our continent, on the continent"

At Macaal we work in a spirit of sharing, mutual support and networking. My dream is to join forces with all the advocates of contemporary African art (foundations, institutions, galleries and curators) in order to create a platform that defends, supports and promotes art from our continent, on the continent. I want us to work hand in hand, unifying our voices to build a strong and engaged base. Beyond being a universal language, art is a liberating platform in which there are no boundaries. Creating a large network in Africa will give its next generation of artists, critics and curators the chance to develop and secure their dreams in their homeland while making their initiatives durable.

The only downside is that, although in the West museums have become a mainstream source of enjoyment and entertainment, in Morocco art and culture are still considered elitist. That's why our main mission at Macaal – besides promoting art and culture – is to democratise access to it with engaging exhibitions, workshops and events throughout the year. Breaking this image, dusting it off, showing a young, lively art world that is accessible to all: this is a full-time job but one that's already beginning to yield results. — (M)

ABOUT THE WRITER: Othman Lazraq is the director of Fondation Alliances, a not-for-profit that focuses on cultural development in Morocco. He is also president of the Musée d'Art Contemporain Africain Al Maaden.

ESSAY 03

Playing to pay
Haggling: a dramatic performance

———

Think you can simply saunter into a stall and purchase whatever takes your fancy? Guess again. In Morocco, the art of the deal involves playing your role to perfection.

by Melkon Charchoglyan, Monocle

You've seen the lamp, the rug, the talisman; spotted it within an Aladdin's cave of spices, faux elephant tusks and *babouches*. There it is, the saucy thing, winking at you. And here's the kindly old salesman sipping sugary mint tea, brilliant in his woollen kaftan and with a smile like a keyboard. Just check the price tag and settle the bill. What could be simpler?

Oh you fool! How I pity your naivety! You've gravely misunderstood the situation. It will almost always culminate in a handshake and an exchange of money as the salesman tells you you've scored the best deal of your life. But is he lying? Between you and the item you desire lies nothing less than an odyssey of wild gesturing, indignation and some serious negotiation. There's no such thing as a price tag in Morocco, certainly not in the souks (and definitely not in a taxi – but that's another story). Whatever you're buying, it'll have to be bartered for.

Haggling is an essential part of daily life here. Not only does it show respect when making a large purchase (making the effort to bargain means you really want the thing) but it's also a bit of sport. Alternatively, you could see it as an *opera buffa*, a piece of comic theatre. Dramatis personae: an overly polite tourist and a canny salesman. You'll have to learn your lines if that charming little carafe is ever to appear in your kitchen. Now let the curtain rise.

Act 1: Enter the tourist. The item you desire beckons; the salesman has seen your interest. Be still my heart. You may feel an initial impulse to launch into brazen action – "I will pay you one dirham, that is my final offer!" – or to make overly eager inquiries. Both will give away your hand. Naturally, we don't always know the real value of an item – how much is a leather ottoman actually worth? – but try to first size up the thing, and the amount you're willing to pay, with a cool head.

Following some pleasantries, questions, compliments and frowning, the salesman will try to convince you that you've chanced on a treasure. In fact, the enamel bracelet you're holding is an 8th-century antique from the Kingdom of Fez – "nothing quite like it in all of Morocco, I assure you" – but he's willing to part with it for a pittance seeing as you're such good friends: 2,000MAD. Don't lose your nerve. Just show some humorous incredulity that conveys the message: "I am not a fool." Raising one eyebrow may help.

Now it's time for the pivotal scene. Name a price that's roughly half of what you're willing to pay and steel yourself.

Act 2: The gauntlet has been thrown down. The souk feels eerily silent as you wonder whether you've committed a gross faux pas. The salesman is shocked and humiliated. He begins to pace back and forth, frowning and gesturing with open palms as he questions your sanity. "Look at this bracelet. Look at it, my friend. Are you not familiar with 8th-century antiques? It clearly belongs in the British Museum." He vacillates between pitying laughter – your ignorance of archaeology is a joke – and furious threats to end the conversation immediately, lest you disgrace him further. If you're able to withstand this onslaught – either with logic ("Old does not mean antique"), pretensions of experience ("Sir, you are speaking to a professor of archaeology and a seasoned buyer of bracelets") or pleas of poverty ("That's all I have, *mon cher*") – you're in with a chance.

> *"There is no such thing as a price tag in Morocco. Whatever you're buying, it'll have to be bartered for"*

Act 3: The bartering begins. Numbers fly faster than at a stock exchange. The salesman will make a counteroffer, attempting to entice you with descending figures. Every trader at the souk has his own technique. Most will simply push the item into your chest and say, "*Yalla*, ok, 1,000MAD and we shake on it." Others are more creative. One salesman in Marrakech forces buyers into something resembling a game of noughts and crosses: he writes a figure, you cross it out, write your own and vice versa for several iterations until a price is agreed.

This is the climactic moment. You've one shot to deliver a flawless performance.

Don't mess it up. Hand the item back with a polite *shoukran* (thank you) – and move to the exit in an affected show of indifference. The audience can't bear to look; the chorus gasps in disbelief. Who will come out on top?

If your acting is Broadway-worthy, the salesman will be ensnared, and in a show of exaggerated defeat he'll succumb to your price. It's a figure, he claims, so abysmally low that his family will never eat again. But he'll do this deal for you, because he's taken a particular liking to you and because he's feeling generous, he claims.

The lights dim; the despondent salesman returns to his cup of sugary mint tea. Exit the tourist, triumphant, exuberant, clutching the precious bracelet. And for just 200MAD. What a steal!

The curtain drops. — (M)

ABOUT THE WRITER: Melkon Charchoglyan is MONOCLE's assistant Books editor. While arguing with salesmen in the souks, he was delighted to sharpen his French and realised an aptitude for the dramatic that he never knew he had.

ESSAY 04
Travel tips
Local know-how

Marrakech can be a sensory overload for first-time visitors so let us help you make sense of it all, from advice for female travellers to what to expect during Ramadan.

*by Aida Alami,
writer*

Marrakech is a popular destination for obvious reasons: around every corner and down every alley lie surprising discoveries. The Red City's heat, colours and flavourful food all add up to a sensory kaleidoscope. But it can also be a challenging destination and it often takes a while to adjust to the way things operate here. Modern nightlife venues coexist with superb centuries-old mosques, magnificent palaces and one of the oldest markets in the world.

As a Marrakech native I know this all too well. So keep your wits about you, yes, but also come with an open mind. And read on for some basic rules that will help you navigate this most bewitching city more smoothly.

Street harassment

Women travelling to Morocco for the first time often ask: "Is it a safe place for us to travel alone?" My response is this: absolutely. Tens of thousands of women do so without issue every year and the Moroccan authorities are especially protective of solo female travellers. It's important to remember that all sexual harassment – be it on the street or over the phone – is against the law.

Having said that, verbal harassment is real and, to be blunt, an inconvenience. Many men are inclined to make inappropriate comments about passing women, no matter what they're wearing (you may choose to avoid revealing tops and short hemlines). But don't let that deter you from exploring on foot.

It's also worth remembering that in Morocco the streets replace bars and clubs as a place for pairing up. Many female residents go to the hairdresser, apply make-up and don beautiful outfits before heading out, in the hope of male attention.

Men too may find themselves the target of unwanted advances from over-eager stallholders hoping to sell their wares. Again it's often harmless and sometimes the best thing to do is say no, thank you, and smile.

Ramadan

During the fasting month of Ramadan (which takes place

"During the fasting month of Ramadan, Muslims don't eat, drink or smoke cigarettes from sunrise to sunset. It can be an interesting time to travel as you'll witness the spiritual side of the country"

at different times because it's in accordance with the lunar calendar), Muslims don't eat, drink or smoke cigarettes from sunrise to sunset. It can be an interesting time to travel as you'll witness the spiritual side of the country. People stay out late into the night, conversing in cafés, and you get to eat pastries that aren't produced during the rest of the year, such as the *chebakia* (a honey-and-sesame cookie). Of course, there's no obligation for non-Moroccans to observe Ramadan, and alcohol is usually served to visitors in high-end bars and restaurants at any time of year.

Visiting mosques

If you aren't Muslim, you aren't permitted to enter a mosque. One of the only exceptions is the Hassan II mosque in Casablanca, which was built on the edge of the Atlantic Ocean in 1993. The same rule applies to most mausoleums. If you are Muslim, dress modestly; women are sometimes asked to cover their shoulders or hair.

Hammams

If you opt for a traditional hammam, you'll find yourself in a large steam room full of naked women or men (feel free to wear a swimsuit if you prefer). Full-body scrubs are available, often for a small fee. The hammams in upmarket hotels usually offer a range of treatment options that make use of clay, henna and argan oil.

I haven't met a single person who has travelled to Morocco and not fallen in love with it. The unwanted attention can be frustrating at times but on the whole the warmth of the people outshines it. Moroccans tend to be exceptionally hospitable. They love practising foreign languages and share a cultural pride in making visitors feel at home. So, my final piece of advice? Just embrace it. It may be overwhelming at times but it's also a delight for all the senses. — (M)

ABOUT THE WRITER: Aida Alami is a Marrakech-based reporter. She's frequently on the road, reporting from north Africa, France and the Caribbean for publications such as *The New York Times*, *NYR Daily* and *Al Jazeera English*.

ESSAY 05

Pay it Sam
Financial harbour

———

A lack of natural charms may have kept Casablanca off the tourist map but its importance as Morocco's economic engine shouldn't be overlooked. The port city has a rich heritage to share with those prepared to delve deeper.

by Meredith Hindley, writer

"The pungent combination of fish, oil and salt that drifts over the city on a hot day is the smell of money. Casablanca is the largest port in Africa on the Atlantic and goods from all over the world pass through it"

I was standing in a shop near the port of Casablanca looking at postcards when the owner approached me in an agitated state. "Madam, are you with the ship?" he asked in French. "Ship?" I queried. "The tour group from the ship – they have left. You will miss it!" He was relieved when I told him I wasn't with the group. There aren't many pale-skinned redheads in Casablanca, which is why he thought I was part of the cruise-ship excursion that had ventured into town for a few hours. He was even more surprised when I told him my nationality. "We don't get many Americans here," he said.

Despite lending its name to the beloved Hollywood film, Casablanca isn't a tourist destination. Those who find themselves here are often simply passing through the port or international airport. Other than the jaw-dropping Hassan II mosque perched next to the Atlantic Ocean, Casablanca's architectural wonders hardly compare to those in Fez, Tangier and Marrakech. Instead, the city is the heart of Morocco's economy.

Dar el-Beida, as the Moroccans call it, began as a sleepy fishing village almost 1,000 years ago. In the Middle Ages, Spanish and Portuguese sailors sought refuge here, their eyes scanning the coast for the "white houses" that inspired the town's name. Casablanca also became a hideout for the pirates who picked off the ships sailing to and from European colonies in the Americas. Tired of coming under attack, the Portuguese levelled the city in 1468 and in the early 16th century built a *kasbah* (fortress) overlooking the harbour. (You're now singing The Clash song, aren't you?).

The Portuguese abandoned Morocco in the 18th century but the Europeans kept coming. As Tangier grew into the largest port in the country and the jewel of the Moroccan coastline, Casablanca remained its ugly step-sister. It lacked the lush greenery and oasis feel of the Mediterranean coastal cities. Travellers who disembarked in Casablanca to go inland to Fez and Marrakech never dallied too long. But the ramshackle nature of the town made it a magnet for people looking to change their luck. European adventurers and disinherited sons came to make their fortunes from shady import-export deals, while Moroccans desperate to escape subsistence living provided brute-force labour at slave wages.

As the money poured in, so too did respectability. By the late 1800s, Casablanca had begun to shake off its reputation as the wild west of Morocco. European trading firms flocked to the city, drawn to the port and the lack of rules that governed commerce in other Moroccan cities, turning Casablanca into a boomtown.

It would only get bigger. The Treaty of Fez (1912) gave France control of Casablanca but not Tangier, which became an "international zone". Frustrated at losing out, the French decided to give Casablanca a makeover. They built a modern port capable of handling cargo vessels and cruise ships so they could funnel Morocco's natural resources out and tourists in. Beautiful posters beckoned travellers to dock at Casablanca. The French also remade the city itself. A wall went up around the medina, hiding away its twisty passages and the Moroccans who lived there. Outside the wall, the French built a new colonial city of whitewashed art deco apartment blocks and boulevards lined with palm trees, cafés and boulangeries. Between 1916 and 1927, Casablanca's population blossomed from

67,000 to 120,000 as Europeans, mainly French, poured in. By the eve of the Second World War, Casablanca was home to 350,000 people.

This colonial Casablanca – with its cafés, gendarmes and Vichy collaborators – is the historical setting for *Casablanca* (1942). Rick's Café Americain was a creation of Warner Brothers' backlot but if you want to live the fantasy, drop by the modern Rick's Café. Under the swirling fans you can order a cocktail and listen

to jazz while imagining you're part of the French resistance. If you like your entertainment more authentic, head to Hôtel Transatlantique, a favourite drinking hole of Allied spies during the war. The hotel's owner refused to let rooms to Nazis.

The Moroccans claimed their country back from the French in 1956 but France's vision of Casablanca as an economic engine remains. The pungent combination of fish, oil and salt that drifts over the city from the port on a hot day is the smell of money. Today, Casablanca is among the largest ports in Africa on the Atlantic and goods from all over the world pass through it daily.

Now home to more than three million people, the city is once again getting a makeover. On Place Mohammed V, which used to be the seat of French power, a new arts and theatre complex has opened. The modern tramway winds its way through the beginnings of a tech corridor. A new high-speed railway connects Casablanca to Tangier in just over two hours, with plans in the works to extend the line to Marrakech.

Casablanca is where Morocco looks to the future but traces of its past remain. If you find yourself passing through – hopefully on a day graced with a glorious cobalt-blue north African sky – squint past the tramway, the satellite dishes and neon signs. Stand on the ramparts and aim a canon at an approaching enemy, while marvelling at the massive operation of the Casablanca port. Slip through the wall into the old medina and follow its passageways, before emerging into the old colonial city where street cafés still reign. — (M)

ABOUT THE WRITER: Meredith Hindley is the author of *Destination Casablanca: Exile, Espionage, and the Battle for North Africa in World War II.*

ESSAY 06
Wheel deal
Driving in Morocco
————

The best way to see the country is by car, so rent yourself a Land Cruiser and follow the lead of our intrepid senior editor. Oh, and perhaps best to take out some cash before you leave.

by Robert Bound, Monocle

In Morocco, get a car and drive. Marrakech is a loud sprawl of a city, a thing of arabesques and intricacy and dirty detail to inspect on foot, but exploring the whole country's just fine at 60 miles an hour. I mean, it's that or take a decade off work to do it in sandals.

Your best bet is to hire a big boy, a Land Cruiser, so that you can push on the highways if it comes to shove. Plus, big tyres help ensure those scorpions don't sting your average speed too hard and riding high in the cab gives you the scope to avoid wild dogs, wild-eyed goats and trouble. We'll come back to the trouble.

Your route? Well, you'll know where you want to go but I'd head to the sea to see Essaouira for a spell and to stock up on road-trip essentials – it's amazing what you can procure down in those portside bars. Next, drive south (and fast) to see some desert, and stay in it for maybe a night or two. Then veer east where the landscape begins to resemble the Grand Canyon, a geology lesson, like valley after valley of forgotten kings. That's a start. Tangier, too, where you'll wish you'd rented a Rolls-Royce Corniche. Until you come to lock it up at night, of course.

In Morocco, a day's drive can take you from city to coast to mountains and then on to midnight at the oasis, if you so desire. Zoom-zoom. You'll be missing much in the way of subtlety and you won't fall into many games of cards with the locals, or get much more than a single suntanned forearm this way, but there's a certain satisfaction in seeing the map shrink as the hot roads are swallowed beneath you and the horizon shimmers like a breeze upon a lake. To do it this way, to get there fast, means speed and that's where the

"The first time you get stopped by the Moroccan traffic police it's good to be sensible. Don't smile. Don't think it's a joke. Imagine a picture dictionary definition of 'contrition' and assume something like its silhouette"

trouble comes in. Hello trouble, my old friend.

The first time you get stopped by the Moroccan traffic police it's good to be sensible. Don't smile. Don't think it's a joke. Imagine a picture dictionary definition of "contrition" and assume something like its silhouette. I mean, I was speeding but this wasn't about anything acquired in that Essaouira bar, I just mean *I was driving too fast*. The traffic police are exceedingly grave, appealingly haughty and fastidiously well-groomed in their grey breeches with the knife-edge creases. Then they give you the charge sheet: it's a killer, it's like a poem by Longfellow; an artefact you just know was greedily inherited from the deathless intricacies of French bureaucracy. And it comes with a 400MAD fine, which is kinda fine. But, as I say, that's the first time.

There's a subtlety to this, a gamble in getting pulled over by the police. When you pay the 400MAD your man might just tell you, as mine did, that on presentation of the paperwork you'll be exonerated from all further traffic infringements for the following 24 hours. It seems fair enough to me but then I'm not a north African lawmaker, nor any sort of lawmaker. So you can imagine. Land Cruiser meet Land Speed Record. And the gamble? Well, if you get pulled over your bad lieutenant might ask if you'd like to save on the paperwork and

just pay 200MAD, which – surely just for convenience – is slipped straight into the smart grey-trouser pocket. Cost effective and deadly efficient I'm sure you'll agree but without the paperwork, the receipt, the *proof*, you could keep getting stung forever and ever, amen.

By the second, third, sixth time you still don't get careless and you don't get insouciant, if you're wise. You can venture a rueful smile and it'll be met with one but that's it. It's serious, OK? The final time, on a wet mountain pass, I was caught for "dangerously" overtaking a car that was driving far more dangerously than I was: I just *had* to get past that madman. I explained it to the officer and there was a shrug and a little smile. "I'm in a hurry," I said. "That I can see, sir," said he. "200?" "Of course." "Thank you." "Not at all, sir. *Bonne journée*." In Morocco, though, still just get a car and drive. Just maybe a little more slowly next time. — (M)

ABOUT THE WRITER: Robert loves a road trip and has an impressive collection of dusty and dog-eared maps to prove it. His packing essentials are mostly legal and feature a fully loaded "classic" iPod, a huge bag of pick'n'mix and Parisienne cigarettes (gifts for kids and adults alike). Amid the slow-moving traffic of London, Robert is MONOCLE's senior editor.

Things we'd buy
—— Exotic souvenirs

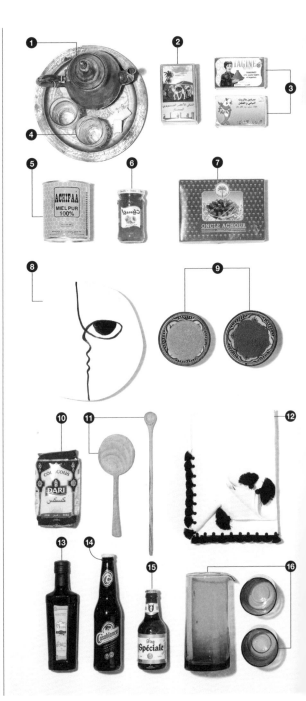

Few countries offer the sheer retail delight of Morocco. From haggling in souks for a winsome vintage tea set or a vibrant ceramic platter, to diving deep into a rug emporium stacked floor to rafters for that one-of-a-kind centrepiece, shopping is a bit like an endurance sport – it takes effort but it's a whole lot of fun and the rewards are many.

Here are our top picks of what to stuff in your suitcase, from contemporary homeware and classic vinyl to aromatic spices that will evoke memories every time you sprinkle them on your food. Whatever you do, when it comes to packing, make sure you leave plenty of room.

01 Vintage tea set from Souk des Tailleurs de Pierre *(Marrakech)*
02 Société Marocaine du Thé et du Sucre tea from Chabi Chic *chabi-chic.com (Marrakech)*
03 Tinned sardines *(nationwide)*
04 Traditional tea glasses *(nationwide)*
05 Honey by Achifaa *(nationwide)*
06 Apricot jam by Delicia *(nationwide)*
07 Dates by Oncle Achour *(nationwide)*
08 Ceramic plate by Malakut *+212 (0)6 4205 6028 (Marrakech)*
09 Spices from Rahba Lakdima *(Marrakech)*
10 Couscous by Dari *(nationwide)*
11 Michi wooden cutlery from 36 Mouassine *36 Rue Mouassine (Marrakech)*
12 Linen by V Barkowski *valeriebarkowski.com (Marrakech)*
13 Nafisa olive oil from Organic Kitchen *organickitchen.ma (Casablanca)*
14 Beer by Casablanca *(nationwide)*
15 Beer by Flag Spéciale *(nationwide)*
16 Glassware from Souk des Tailleurs de Pierre *(Marrakech)*
17 Scarf by Malakut *+212 (0)6 4205 6028 (Marrakech)*
18 Le Chapelier hat from 33 Rue Majorelle *33ruemajorelle.com (Marrakech)*
19 Argan oil by Maison d'Asa *maisondasa.com (Casablanca)*
20 L'Art du Bain honey soap from 33 Rue Majorelle *33ruemajorelle.com (Marrakech)*
21 Héritage Berbère cologne from Max & Jan *maxandjan.com (Marrakech)*
22 Corinne Bensimon vase from 36 Mouassine *36 Rue Mouassine (Marrakech)*

23 Shirts by Marrakshi Life
marrakshilife.com (Marrakech)
24 Vase by Bouchra Boudoua
+212 (0)6 6120 7695
25 Sandals by LRNCE
lrnce.com (Marrakech)
26 *Babouches* by Soul
Marrakech
*+212 (0)6 5342 9808
(Marrakech)*
27 Backgammon board and
ceramic tile by Popham Design
pophamdesign.com (Marrakech)
28 *Sahara* (1977) by
Abdelwahab Doukkali from
6 Souk Jeld
*+212 (0)6 7128 2128
(Marrakech)*
29 Scented candle by
Rumi 1436
43 Rue Amrah (Tangier)
30 YSL matches from
Max & Jan
maxandjan.com (Marrakech)
31 Vintage Berber rug from
Les Nomades de Marrakech
*lesnomadesdemarrakech.com
(Marrakech)*
32 Postcard from Maison
de la Photographie
*maisondelaphotographie.ma
(Marrakech)*
33 Hand of Fatima from
Souk Semmarine
(Marrakech)
34 *Un pays pour mourir*
by Abdellah Taïa from
Librairie des Colonnes
54 Avenue Pasteur (Tangier)
35 *The Sheltering Sky* by Paul
Bowles from Les Insolites
28 Khalid Ibn El Oualid (Tangier)
36 Cushion cover by LRNCE
lrnce.com (Marrakech)
37 Tote by Cinémathèque
de Tanger
3 Rue de la Liberté (Tangier)
38 Hand-painted sign
citywide (Marrakech)
39 *Photography, Fashion,
Film, Design* by Hassan Hajjaj
from Riad Yima
riadyima.com (Marrakech)

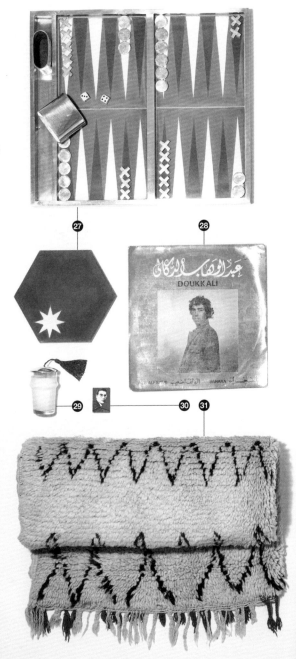

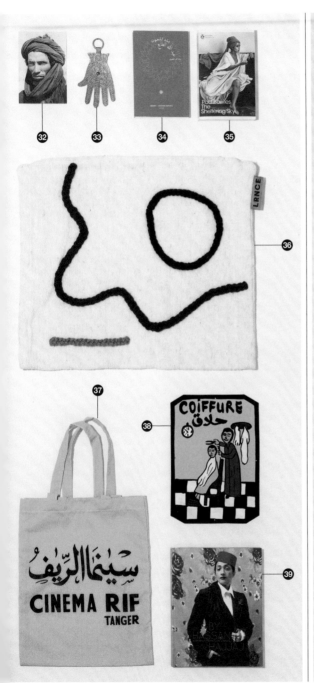

Shopping in the souks

Marrakech's medina can look like one great big souk so it might seem counterintuitive to talk about individual markets. But within the endless warren of stall-lined streets are specific hubs, several of which specialise in one trade. Locating them can be tricky (ask around) and finding your way out can prove even more difficult – but that's part of the adventure. Here's a rundown of our favourites.

01 Souk Semmarine: One of the main souks in the medina, effectively acting as a thoroughfare and entrance to other markets. Here you'll find everything from spices and pastries to textiles, lamps and leather goods.

02 Souk des Tailleurs de Pierre: This souk, which runs from near Rahba Lakdima through to Rue Mouassine, was originally the masons' market. Today the masons are few but you'll find excellent brass goods and glassware (such as the short hand-blown glasses you might find in your riad), among other items.

03 Souk des Teinturiers: Also known as Souk Sebbaghine. This is the dyers' market, where textiles are coloured in saffron, indigo, cobalt and every other shade imaginable. If you're after raw materials (such as wool for knitting), you've come to the right place.

Resources
— Marrakech

Transport
Make your move

01 Flights: Aéroport Marrakech Ménara, which opened a new terminal in 2016, is just 5km from the city. We recommend organising a pick-up through your riad or hotel since taking a taxi will involve heavy haggling.

02 Trains: Train travel from Marrakech used to be a painful affair but new links to Casablanca have cut the journey time down to just over two-and-a-half hours. Trains leave more or less every hour and are quite comfortable. From there you can hop on the high-speed Al Boraq trains (named after the mythical beast that the Prophet Muhammad rides in the Quran), which get you to Tangier in two hours.

03 Taxis: Taxis are the principal form of transport in the city as there's little public transport. Follow our handy tips for easy riding (see page 13).

04 On foot: Marrakech is surprisingly small and you can cross the medina in under an hour (providing you don't get lost). Walking to the other neighbourhoods, however, is another matter. We'd suggest hailing a taxi to both Gueliz and Hivernage.

Reading list
Page turners

01 Lawrence Osborne, 'The Forgiven' (2012): This haunting novel follows a wealthy British couple who kill a boy in the Moroccan desert and try to cover it up – with dire consequences.

02 Laila Lalami, 'Hope and Other Dangerous Pursuits' (2005): Interconnected short stories that explore immigration today, concerning the lives of four Moroccans.

03 Driss Chraïbi, 'The Simple Past' (1954): Driss Chraïbi's brooding coming-of-age-story sees two generations clash in colonial Morocco.

Language
Essential Arabic

01 Salam Al'aikoum: Hello (formal; literally "may peace be upon you")

02 Marhaba: Welcome or hello (informal)

03 Shoukran: Thank you

04 La'a: No

05 Na'am: Yes

06 Aafak: Please

07 Inshallah: Let's hope so or we'll see (literally "God willing")

08 Alhamdulillah: Praise God (said when something good has happened, or just to say that you're fine)

09 Beslama: Goodbye

Events
Morocco-wide

01 1-54 Contemporary African Art Fair, Marrakech: Touria El Glaoui's stellar fair celebrates African art, with stops in London, New York and, of course, Marrakech. *February; 1-54.com/marrakech*

02 Rallye Maroc Classic, Marrakech: The car rally culminates in Marrakech with much showmanship and engine revving. *March; rallye-maroc-classic.com*

03 Printemps du Livre et des Arts de Tanger, Tangier: This week-long literary festival is organised by the Institut Français and takes on a different theme each year. *April; if-maroc.org*

04 Jazzablanca, Casablanca: The name says it all. A jazz festival around the city (with a few other genres thrown in for good measure). *July; jazzablanca.com*

05 Casa Festival, Casablanca: Live music, theatre and parades that promote Casa's heritage and artistic community. *July; wecasablanca.com*

06 Tangier International Film Festival, Tangier: A celebration of cinema founded by students at Université Abdelmalek Essaâdi. *November; festivaldetanger.com*

07 Festival International du Film de Marrakech, Marrakech: Another film festival promoting north African and global talent, with backing from big actors and Moroccan royals. *November, December; festivalmarrakech.info*

Resources
—— Tangier

Transport
En route

01 Flights: Aéroport Tanger Ibn Battouta is 14km from the city centre. Unfortunately there are no train or bus links so the only option is to hop in a taxi, which takes 25 minutes. The price of a ride into the city is government-controlled and costs 250MAD before 20.00 and 300MAD after.

02 Taxis: Not all taxis in Tangier have meters, and if they don't, make sure you agree on a price before getting in (expect to be charged up to 50 per cent more at night). The taxis here operate a bit like buses, so remember you can flag down one that has passengers but spare seats as long as it's heading the right way.

03 Ferries: Tangier is connected to Tarifa in Spain by ferry, which leaves roughly 16 times a day. The journey takes an hour and costs about 750MAD for passengers travelling by foot.

Must reads
By the book

01 Paul Bowles, 'Let It Come Down' (1952): Written by one of Tangier's most famous expats, this novel tells the story of an American bank clerk who moves to Tangier to start a new life but falls down a path of self-destruction.

02 William Burroughs, 'Naked Lunch' (1959): William Burroughs wrote this literary landmark while living in Tangier. The novel follows the adventures of his alter-ego William Lee, a drug addict fleeing arrest.

03 Tahar Ben Jelloun, 'Leaving Tangier' (2009): Moroccan writer Tahar Ben Jelloun's novel tells the story of a young man called Azel who dreams of, you guessed it, leaving Tangier and starting again in Spain.

Resources
—— Casablanca

Transport
Hitch a ride

01 Flights: Aéroport Casablanca Mohammed V is Morocco's major air hub but beware of flying here from Marrakech: the route is regularly plagued by delays and cancellations, plus it's a further hour by car from the airport to the city centre.

02 Taxis: Many visitors coming to Casa from Marrakech will arrive by taxi (private hire, mind). All in all the journey is no longer than going by train or plane, and costs roughly the same. Once in town, taxis are relatively easy to hail (most of them are red) and more likely to switch on the metre and treat you more fairly than those in Marrakech.

03 Trains: The high-speed Al Boraq links Casa-Voyageurs train station to Tangier and Rabat, with slightly slower trains heading to Marrakech.

04 By foot: Certain parts of Casablanca are pleasantly walkable, including the Habbous, the Ancienne Medina and Derb Omar (particularly around Boulevard Mohammed V). But much of the city is dissected by big highways – if in doubt, hop in a taxi.

Films
The silver screen

01 'Casablanca' (1942): One of the most famous films of mid-century Hollywood – and certainly the film that defines the image of this city, romanticised though it is. Humphrey Bogart plays a heartbroken casino-owner in Vichy-controlled Casablanca. Expect dinner suits, champagne and tearjerking moments.

02 'Attentato ai tre grandi' (1967): Another war-time thriller, in this case actually shot in Morocco (unlike the above). The Italian film, which is known as *Desert Commandos* in English, sees three German soldiers head to Casablanca with a mission to assassinate the top three Allied commanders during the Casablanca Conference of 1943.

About Monocle
—— Step inside

London HQ
——
Our editorial
office is in
Marylebone

In 2007, Monocle was launched as a monthly magazine briefing on global affairs, business, culture, design and much more. We believed there was a globally minded audience of readers who were hungry for opportunities and experiences beyond their national borders.

Today Monocle is a complete media brand with print, audio and online elements – not to mention our expanding network of shops and cafés. Besides our London HQ we have international bureaux in Toronto, Tokyo, Zürich, Hong Kong and Los Angeles, with more on the way. We continue to grow and flourish and at our core is the simple belief that there will always be a place for a print brand that is committed to telling fresh stories and sending photographers on assignments. It's also a case of knowing that our success is all down to the readers, advertisers and collaborators who have supported us along the way.

International bureaux
Boots on the ground

We're based in London and have bureaux in Hong Kong, Tokyo, Zürich, Toronto and Los Angeles, with more to come. We also call upon reports from our contributors in more than 35 cities around the world. For this guide, MONOCLE reporters Joe Pickard, Chloë Ashby, Melkon Charchoglyan and Hester Underhill decamped to Marrakech, Casablanca and Tangier to explore all they have to offer. They also called on contacts to ensure that we've covered the best in food, culture and more.

Online
Digital delivery

We have a dynamic website: *monocle.com.* As well as being the place to hear our radio station, Monocle 24, the site presents our films, which are beautifully shot and edited by our in-house team and provide a fresh perspective on our stories. Check out the films celebrating the cities that make up our Travel Guide Series before you explore the rest of the site.

Retail and cafés
Food for thought

Via our shops in Toronto, Zürich, Tokyo, London, Los Angeles and Hong Kong – including one in the airport (*pictured*) – we sell products that cater to our readers' tastes and are produced in collaboration with brands we believe in. We also have cafés in Tokyo, Zürich and London. And if you are in the UK capital visit the Kioskafé in Paddington, which combines good coffee and great reads.

④

Print
Committed to the page

MONOCLE is published 10 times a year. We also produce two standalone publications – THE FORECAST, packed with insights into the year ahead, and THE ESCAPIST – plus seasonal weekly newspapers and an annual *Drinking & Dining Directory*. Since 2013 we have also been publishing travel guides, like this one, and bigger books. Visit *monocle.com/shop*.

⑤

Radio
Sound approach

Monocle 24 is our round-the-clock radio station that was launched in 2011. It delivers global news and shows covering foreign affairs, urbanism, business, culture, food and drink, design and print media. When you find yourself in Morocco, tune into *The Globalist* for a newsy start to your morning. You can listen live or download any of our shows from *monocle.com*, iTunes or SoundCloud.

Priority service
Subscribers save 10 per cent in our online shop

Join the club

01
Subscribe to Monocle
A subscription is a simple way to make sure that you never miss an issue – and you'll enjoy many additional benefits.

02
Be in the know
Our subscribers have exclusive access to the entire Monocle archive, and priority access to selected product collaborations, at *monocle.com*.

03
Stay in the loop
Subscription copies are delivered to your door at no extra cost no matter where you are in the world. We also offer an auto-renewal service to ensure that you never miss an issue.

04
And there's more...
Subscribers benefit from a 10 per cent discount at all Monocle shops, including online, and receive exclusive offers and invitations to events around the world.

Choose your package

Premium one year
13 × issues
+ Porter Sub Club bag

One year
12 × issues
+ Monocle Voyage tote bag

Six months
6 × issues

Writers
Aida Alami
Chloë Ashby
Robert Bound
Melkon Charchoglyan
James Clark
Meredith Hindley
Othman Lazraq
Joe Pickard
Mandy Sinclair
Hester Underhill

Research
Melkon Charchoglyan
Dan Einav
Audrone Fiodorenko
Zayana Zulkiflee

Special thanks
Imad Dahmani
Aimee Hartley
Louis Harnett O'Meara
Raffael Lienert
Rachel Lucas-Craig
Lahbib El Moumni
Lizzie Porter
Louise Przybylski
Virginie Vaillant
Harry Wong

PICTURES: MARRAKECH

Chief photographer
Andrew Taylor

Photographer
Mark Arrigo

Still life
David Sykes

Images
Alamy
Cyril Boixe
Benoit Bost
Melkon Charchoglyan
David Bloch Gallery
Kasia Gatkowska
Getty Images
Montresso Art Foundation
Joe Pickard
Tania Pnova

Illustrators
Satoshi Hashimoto
Ceylan Sahin
Tokuma

PICTURES: CASABLANCA

Chief photographer
Thomas Humery

Still life
David Sykes

Illustrators
Satoshi Hashimoto
Tokuma

PICTURES: TANGIER

Chief photographer
Thomas Humery

Still life
David Sykes

Illustrators
Satoshi Hashimoto
Tokuma

Monocle
EDITOR IN CHIEF AND
CHAIRMAN
Tyler Brûlé
EDITOR
Andrew Tuck
CREATIVE DIRECTOR
Richard Spencer Powell

**The Monocle Travel Guide
Series: Marrakech, Tangier
+ Casablanca**
GUIDE EDITOR
Melkon Charchoglyan
ASSOCIATE GUIDE EDITORS
Chloë Ashby
Joe Pickard
Hester Underhill
DESIGNER
Giulia Tugnoli
PHOTO EDITOR
Victoria Cagol

**The Monocle Travel Guide
Series**
SERIES EDITOR
Joe Pickard
ASSOCIATE EDITOR
Chloë Ashby
ASSISTANT EDITOR
Melkon Charchoglyan
DESIGNER
Giulia Tugnoli
PHOTO EDITOR
Victoria Cagol

CHAPTER EDITING: MARRAKECH

Need to know
Melkon Charchoglyan

Hotels
Hester Underhill

Food and drink
Mandy Sinclair

Retail
Melkon Charchoglyan

Things we'd buy
Melkon Charchoglyan
Joe Pickard

Essays
Chloë Ashby

Culture
Chloë Ashby

Design and architecture
Joe Pickard

Sport and fitness
Hester Underhill

Walk
Melkon Charchoglyan

Resources
Melkon Charchoglyan

EDITING: TANGIER
Joe Pickard
Hester Underhill

EDITING: CASABLANCA
Chloë Ashby
Melkon Charchoglyan

Marrakech, Tangier + Casablanca
Index

New

The collection
Planning another trip? We have a global suite of guides, from Amsterdam to Zürich. Cities are fun. Let's explore.

Buy today at all good bookshops

You can also visit the online shops at *monocle.com* and *shop.gestalten.com* to get hold of your copies.

Look out for 'The Monocle Guide to Hotels, Inns and Hideaways'